Practical
Cheddar Cheese-making

John Tyler & Sons,

DAIRY ENGINEERS,

Highbridge, Somerset,

Can supply any of the Dairy Utensils illustrated in this book, and Price Lists will be sent free on application.

Information on the fitting up of Dairies will be gladly given to intending purchasers.

With our new pattern Steam Generator the labour of cheese-making is reduced to a minimum.

This Generator will:—

> **MAKE CHEESE**
>
> **BOIL WATER**
>
> **SCALD CHURNS**
>
> **HEAT THE CHEESE ROOM**
>
> **COOK PIGS' FOOD** and
>
> **EJECT WHEY** from the
>
> **DAIRY** to the **PIGGERIES.**

The Auctions held at HIGHBRIDGE every week for the sale of Cheddar and Caerphilly Cheese are the largest in the West of England.

A British Firm
ESTABLISHED 132 YEARS.

R. J. F. & B's World-renowned Dairy Preparations are used and recommended at the principal Dairy Institutes and have the largest sale in Great Britain.

R. J. FULLWOOD & BIAND'S

'STAG' BRAND
ANNATTO

'DAIRY' BRAND
RENNET

'OLEO' Butter Coloring

The BEST is the CHEAPEST to use in the long run.

R. J. F. & B. are the Largest and Oldest Firm of Annatto and Rennet Manufacturers in Great Britain.

R. J. F. & B. hold patents for the manufacture of Rennet.

MANUFACTORY AND OFFICES:
31, 33, & 35 Bevendon Street, HOXTON, LONDON.

Pond & Sons, Ltd.,
BLANDFORD.

Ponds' First Prize Cheddar Cheese Tub and Jacketed Whey Heater.

Makers of :—

CHEESE TUBS	**CURD TINS**
CHEESE VATS	**REFRIGERATORS**
WHEY HEATERS	**CURD KNIVES**
CHEESE PRESSES	**MILK CHURNS**

DAIRY FARMERS

Your Herds of Milch Cows are too valuable to be the subject of experiments.

Milking the 'Manus' way is worth

your personal consideration.

The 'Manus' Milking Machine

COMBINES

SAFETY, SIMPLICITY, CLEANLINESS, RELIABILITY, and all-round **EFFICIENCY.**

The Machine which NEVER fails to give Satisfaction.
Easily operated by Women and Lads.

BOVING and Co., Ltd.,
56 KINGSWAY, LONDON, W.C.

W. H. Smith & Co.,

DAIRY ENGINEERS,

CHEESE-MAKING APPLIANCES OF EVERY DESCRIPTION.

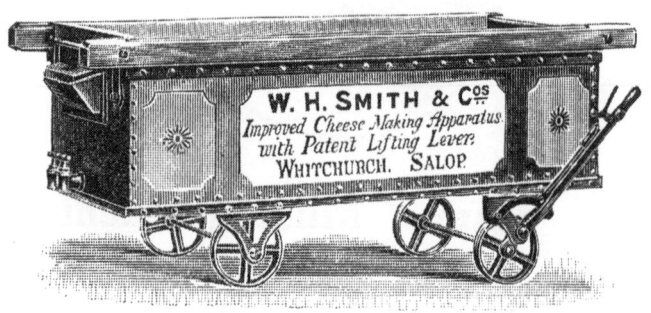

UPWARDS OF 4,000 SOLD.

SEND FOR CATALOGUE.   *POST FREE.*

WORKS,
Whitchurch,
SALOP.

ALL BRITISH

THE 'VACCAR'
Milking Machine.

'To hold the Cow to her milk' is the one basic essential that no milking machine can fall short of and be a success.

This vital requirement has, however, from the earliest day proved the one stumbling block to the success of mechanical milking.

There is only one test in this connexion that is absolutely final—years of continuous and successful use.

The actual facts are that there is only one machine that passes this test—The 'VACCAR,' fitted with EXCLUSIVE MASTER PATENTS.

VACCAR, LTD.,
7 Southwark Street, London, S.E.

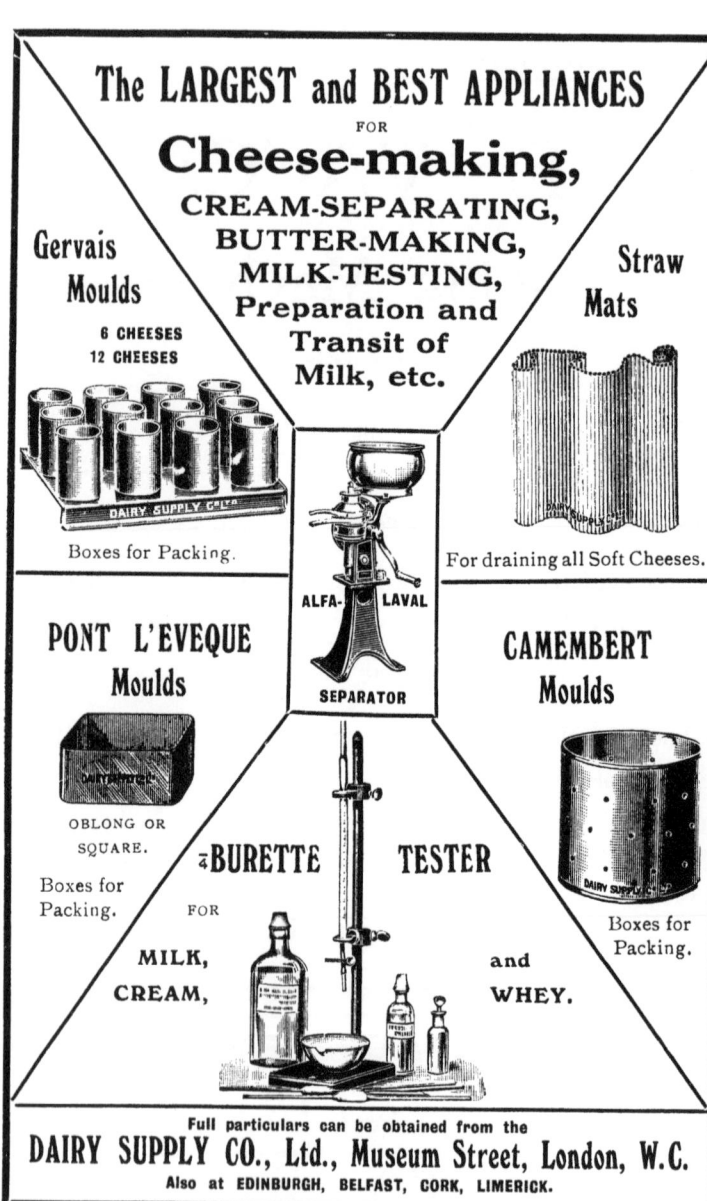

Practical
Cheddar Cheese-making

BY

DORA G. SAKER, N.D.D., B.D.F.D.
(Instructor in Cheese-making under the Somerset County Council)

published on behalf of the BMTBCRC
by Naval and Military Press

Published on behalf of the BMTBCRC by

The Naval & Military Press Ltd
Unit 10 Ridgewood Industrial Park,
Uckfield, East Sussex,
TN22 5QE England

Tel: +44 (0) 1825 749494
Fax: +44 (0) 1825 765701

In reprinting in facsimile from the original, any imperfections are inevitably reproduced and the quality may fall short of modern type and cartographic standards.

PREFACE.

THE primary object of this book on Cheddar cheese-making is, that it may be of assistance to cheese-makers, on farms, or in cheese-making dairies, and to students at dairy schools. Constant repetition will be found in its pages, but the writer has found by experience that important facts require repetition, if they are to be impressed on the mind. The information given is that obtained from a number of years' experience in Cheddar cheese-making, both with small and large quantities of milk, on farms, and in dairies, and while teaching students, and if the advice proves helpful to those encountering difficulties with their cheese, the book will have served its purpose.

DORA G. SAKER.

HARPENDEN,
    HERTS.
February, 1917.

UNITS

To calculate centigrade from fahrenheit:
temperature in centigrade = 5/9 x (temperature in fahrenheit - 32)

Fahrenheit	Centigrade
185	85.0
165	73.9
105	40.6
102	38.9
100	37.8
98	36.7
96	35.6
95	35.0
94	34.4
92	33.3
90	32.2
88	31.1
86	30.0
85	29.4
84	28.9
80	26.7
75	23.9
70	21.1
65	18.3
60	15.6
58	14.4
55	12.8
50	10.0
45	7.2

Rennet is measured in a fluid dram (Imperial) which is one eighth of a fluid ounce (Imperial) or 3.55 ml.

One fluid ounce (Imperial) is 28.4 ml.

One gallon (Imperial) is 4.54 litres

One lb. (Imperial) is 0.45 kg.

One ton (Imperial) is 2,240 lb. and 1,016 kg. (a little over a metric tonne)

There are twenty hundredweight (cwt) in a ton so one hundredweight is 112 lb. (just over 50 kg.)

CONTENTS.

CHAP.		PAGE
I.	VALUE OF CHEESE AS A FOOD. ESSENTIALS FOR THE PRODUCTION OF A UNIFORM ARTICLE	1
II.	THE PRODUCTION OF PURE AND UNIFORM MILK. EFFECT OF SOIL, WATER SUPPLY, AND FOOD AND BREED OF COW	3
III.	DAIRY BUILDINGS AND EQUIPMENT. APPLIANCES . . .	8
IV.	SKILL OF MAKER. THE CONTROL OF ACIDITY AND MOISTURE. ACIDITY TESTS. USE OF STARTER . .	29
V.	THE MAKING OF CHEDDAR CHEESE.	38
VI.	TAINTS AND FAULTS IN CHEESE. THEIR CAUSE, PREVENTION, AND REMEDY	58
VII.	RENNET AND ITS SUBSTITUTES. SALT AND COLORING USED FOR CHEESE	70
VIII.	THE RIPENING OF CHEESE. STORAGE AND PACKING FOR EXPORT AND MARKET	77
IX.	EXHIBITION OF CHEESE. POINTS FOR JUDGING CHEESE. THE KEEPING OF CHEESE RECORDS	80
X.	RETURNS OBTAINED FROM CHEESE-MAKING. BYE-PRODUCTS. WHEY AND WHEY BUTTER.	84
XI.	MAKING CHEESE FROM HEATED OR PASTEURIZED MILK .	89
XII.	YIELD OF CHEESE. STANDARD FOR CHEESE. BUYING MILK FOR CHEESE-MAKING.	92

ILLUSTRATIONS.

PLATES		PAGE
A.	DAIRY, SHOWING MILK COMING INTO VAT BY CHUTE.	*Face* 16
B.	STEAM WHEY LIFTER	,, 17
C.	CURD IN TUB AFTER DRAWING OFF WHEY . . .	,, 32
D.	CURD CUT FOR PILING IN TUB.	,, 33
E.	CURD PILED IN TUB	,, 48
F.	CURD ON COOLER, 1st PACKING	,, 49
G.	,, ,, ,, 2nd ,, ...	,, 64
H.	,, ,, ,, 3rd ,, ...	,, 65
I.	,, ,, ,, 4th ,, ...	,, 80
J.	CURD BEING GROUND OR MILLED.	,, 81
K.	LARGE AND TRUCKLE CHEDDARS IN CHEESE ROOM.	,, 96
L.	CHEESE EN ROUTE FOR DEALER'S STORES . . .	,, 97
	GERBER DIRT TESTER DISCS	4
	STEAM BOILER	13
	OBLONG JACKETED VAT	15
	ROUND TIN TUB	17
	JACKETED TUB	17
	OVERHEAD HEATER	18
	CURD COOLER	19
	AMERICAN CURD KNIVES.	20
	POND'S CURD KNIFE	20
	CURD BREAKER	20
	CURD RAKE	21
	MILK STRAINER	21
	MILK BOWL	21
	CURD MILL	22
	CURD SIEVE	23
	CURD SCOOP.	23
	CURD WHISK	23
	TRUCKLE MOULD	23
	CHEDDAR MOULD	23
	DOUBLE CHEESE PRESS	24
	SINGLE CHEESE PRESS.	25
	DIAGRAM OF CHEESE PRESS	26
	GANG CHEESE PRESS	27
	ACIDIMETER	32

CHAPTER I.

VALUE OF CHEESE AS A FOOD. ESSENTIALS FOR THE PRODUCTION OF A UNIFORM ARTICLE.

VALUE OF CHEESE AS A FOOD.

THE object of cheese-making is to utilize more of the solid matter in milk than is done with butter-making, and to make an article that can be kept for an appreciable length of time. By the manufacture of cheddar cheese, an article of food is made that will keep up to twelve months; in this way the food supplies of the country can be conserved. Cheese has been a well-known article of diet from the earliest times, and it is the foodstuff that most readily takes the place of meat.

According to some authorities, one ounce of cheese is equal in feeding value to one egg, or a glass of milk, or 2 oz. meat, and in normal times, is cheaper in comparison, therefore there can be no question as to the economic value of cheese. Cheese, like many of the common foods, is complex in composition and varies according to the different processes it undergoes during manufacture. The chief objection brought forward against the consumption of cheese, is that of indigestibility. This is no doubt true of some varieties, but these are the highly-ripened or seasoned kinds, intended to be used only in small quantities as a condiment. The mild-flavored cheese, or those not highly ripened, are those usually selected for eating in quantity, and, as a substitute for meat.

In the mining districts of this country, large quantities of caerphilly, and other 'green' or fresh cheese are consumed, and can be eaten with bread in almost equal quantities. Owing to the softness of the texture, this cheese is easily assimilated, and for workers underground does not cause excessive heat in the system.

Hard cheese such as cheddar, consisting of fat, proteid and water in equal parts offers considerable resistance to the digestive juices, when swallowed in small lumps. The fatty particles form a covering over the rest of the substance, and hinder the ferments of digestion from readily dissolving it. On the other hand, if well masticated, so that the digestive fluids can come into thorough contact with its constituents, cheese is readily digestible, and should give no trouble on this account, if eaten in conjunction with food which requires mastication, sufficient juices are secreted to assist the digestive processes. Cheese can also be made more digestible if grated finely and served with milk or cream. The fact that cheese does not contain starch, suggests that like meat, it should be combined with bread, potatoes and other starchy foods, and with vegetables and sweets. It has been estimated that the amount of cheese consumed in this country in normal times is between $10\frac{1}{2}$ and $13\frac{1}{2}$ lb. per unit, per annum. Of this 6.8 lb. comes from abroad, and 3.7 lb. is manufactured here. Of the imported cheese, just under a half comes from Canada, the other from New Zealand, Holland, United States, France, and Belgium. It has been calculated that it would require 9 per cent of the milk produced in this country to provide the necessary quantity of cheese required for home consumption.

Essentials for the Production of Uniform Cheese.

1. The raw material, namely milk, must be obtained under the best conditions.
2. The buildings and equipment must be suitable to the work that is to be carried on.
3. The maker must be skilful, and work to produce the best only.
4. There must be complete control of the direct process for the variety of cheese made.
5. The ripening and after-treatment of the cheese must be in accordance with its requirements.

CHAPTER II.

THE PRODUCTION OF PURE AND UNIFORM MILK. EFFECT OF SOIL, WATER SUPPLY, AND FOOD AND BREED OF COW.

HIGH-CLASS cheese cannot be produced from inferior and dirty milk. Taints may to some extent be overcome, but the resulting product will never possess the market value of one made from pure milk. The milk must be obtained under the most cleanly and sanitary conditions. For this reason attention must be given to the ventilation, regular lime-washing and cleaning of the byres, grooming of the cows, cleanliness in all milking operations and of utensils. The removal of the milk from the byre as soon as obtained prevents the absorption of odors and the immediate straining, aeration, and cooling in a clean atmosphere retards the development of injurious organisms present.

In order that milk may not deteriorate rapidly, and to make good cheese, it must be freed from any impurities it may contain. Apart from visible dirt, there are innumerable fine particles that cannot be seen unless the milk stands for any length of time, and these must be removed by some straining process.

When milk is put through a dirt centrifuge, all the dirt is driven out, but this method is practically impossible in an ordinary farm-house dairy (although of great assistance in factories) and the only available method is straining. Cotton-wool filters are most efficient, but unfortunately these are rarely used, sieves of various kinds are more popular, as the milk runs through them more rapidly. Sieves, whether of wire gauze or perforated metal, are inefficient by themselves and should be used in conjunction with some material; they will remove the larger particles, and if a cloth is tied outside the sieve the finer part of the dirt can be taken from the milk. The materials in use vary considerably, in cheese-making districts cheese-grey of varying thickness is employed, but it allows a great deal of dirt to pass through. The best strainer cloth for ordinary use is cheap flannelette, which more nearly resembles the cotton-wool discs that are used in the best strainers, as the fluffiness keeps back more of the fine sediment and hairs. Milk tested for dirt after being strained through flannelette shows much less dirt than with other materials. Added to this advantage, it is cheaper and will last quite as long as any other material and is no more difficult to wash after use, if first rinsed in cold water.

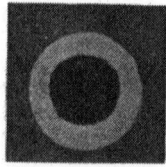 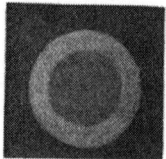

GERBER DIRT TESTER DISCS, SHOWING THE DIFFERENCE BETWEEN A PINT OF STRAINED AND UNSTRAINED MILK.

Milk is usually cleanest when the cows are milked in the fields, except in wet weather when the rain washes the dirt from their bodies and the drainings fall into the milk.

The quality and quantity of the milk yielded is greatly influenced by various factors. We may take first, the breed of cows. The milk from any breed may be made into cheese, but when the economic value for that purpose is taken into account some breeds prove more suitable than others. Shorthorn and its crosses, and Ayrshire cows are the most popular animals. The globules of fat in the milk of these breeds are smaller than in others, and they become more easily entangled with the casein when the milk is curdled, thus producing a more even curd. Jersey and Guernsey milk may be made into cheese and a larger yield is obtained, but care must be taken in the manufacture or great loss of fat will ensue. Holland, the home of the Holstein, has always been noted

CHEDDAR CHEESE-MAKING.

for its cheese-making factories, but the yield per gallon from this breed is not great as the milk does not always contain a high percentage of fat. Whatever the breed, healthy cows should be selected and bred with a view to using their milk for cheese-making.

On most cheese-making farms it is usually preferable to have the cows coming in to milk in the early spring of the year, especially when winter feed is scarce. But where it is required to make cheese all the year round, and therefore to have a regular milk supply, the cows should come in as follows, for the quarters commencing—

1 quarter Sept. 35 p.c. will have dry 17 p.c. in milk 92 p.c.
2 ,, Jan. 30 p.c. ,, 18 p.c. ,, 91 p.c.
3 ,, Mar. 18 p.c. ,, 30 p.c. ,, 85 p.c.
4 ,, June 17 p.c. ,, 35 p.c. ,, 83 p.c.

Thus the lowest number of cows in milk is in Spring and early Summer, when the fresh grass is likely to cause an increase in the yield.

The food of the cow influences not only the quantity, but also the quality of the milk, both as regards richness and suitability for cheese-making. Most cheese is turned out when the main food of the cow is grass, but when made early and late, that is before the cows go out to grass, and when the pastures become scanty, other foods have to be given in addition. The best pastures in the country produce sufficient herbage to keep a cow to every two acres, but with poor pastures 3½-4 acres may be necessary. *[stocking rate]*

Foods liable to taint the milk must be fed sparsely, or not at all; succulent foods such as clover, green maize, vetches, rape, etc., fed in excess produce milk causing the cheese to have a distinct taste and odor. Some foods of an oily nature produce a milk that readily loses its fat during the process of cheese-making, therefore with them other foods must be fed to balance the ration.

With care a good cheese can be obtained from the milk of cows fed on artificial foods, one that will keep without going off flavor, but there is no doubt that the best cheese is produced with less trouble from pasture grass.

Good pastures are found on many different soils, but the

finest are usually on a good formation, such as red sandstone and limestone, they have the greatest productive power for the useful grasses and leguminous plants. Pastures to produce the most satisfactory milk must be free from injurious weeds, which crowd out the useful grasses, and they should contain a high proportion of the long-lived species to prevent deterioration. Badly drained soils produce rank herbage, utterly unsuitable for milk production.

The presence of a large proportion of lime in the soil produces a milk giving a firmer and better curd, thus a great benefit is derived by dressing a soil that is deficient in lime (about 2 tons per acre).

A high percentage of nitrogen in the soil causes the cows to scour, and thus there is a greater risk of contaminated milk. This has been found in what are known locally as the 'teart' lands of Somerset.

Rich pastures produce more milk, lower in acidity and quality than poor pastures. Milk from such pastures is often deficient in casein and less acidity must be developed throughout the process of cheese-making. Milk from limestone and red sandstone develops acidity slowly, that from heavy loams and clays quickly.

It is singular that the texture of the curd from milk obtained off different soils can, in many instances, be compared with the soil. Thus on clay land the curd retains its moisture and requires a higher scald to get rid of it, while with a loose sandy soil, the curd dries too rapidly.

Pastures should afford some shelter for the cows both from excessive heat in summer and from cold winds in spring and autumn, or there will be a decided shrinkage in the milk.

Too much stress cannot be laid upon the importance of a pure water supply in the production of good milk, as without it good milk is impossible.

Water for cleansing purposes must be pure and free from sediment, and a plentiful supply is of the utmost importance in cleansing dairy utensils; cold water is also necessary to cool the evening's milk in the hot weather.

As regards the drinking water for the cows it has been estimated that they require six gallons per day, 5 lb. for every 1 lb. of milk produced. It is found in practice that they prefer soft water and if there is a pure and plentiful supply they should be given it in preference to hard. Soft water when given to the cows produces milk from which the curd, when made into cheese, requires to be scalded higher. Too much iron in the water decreases the flow of milk.

Sluggish pools and ditches are undesirable, as the cows, wading in them in hot weather, contaminate the water with their manure, which, clinging to their udders and flanks eventually finds its way into the milk.

When the pastures are bordered with streams, attention should be given that the places where the cows drink do not become foul and boggy, through their trampling down the edges; if this happens the place should be railed off and a fresh entrance made. In this way much tainted cheese is avoided.

Where the cows drink from troughs fed from the main, a ball-cock should be affixed so that a constant stream of fresh water is available.

CHAPTER III.

DAIRY BUILDINGS AND EQUIPMENT. APPLIANCES.

DAIRY BUILDINGS.

These should have if possible a northern aspect, and be far removed from the proximity of the piggeries, manure heaps, food stores, etc. When a separate building, the dairy should be built on a higher level than the farm buildings, so that it cannot be contaminated with drainage from the farm-yard; when forming part of the dwelling-house it is usually higher, except in the case of very old-fashioned homesteads. Arrangements should be made to provide an even temperature, as this is one of the great essentials in cheese-making. For the roof of the buildings tiles are better than slates, as they are not so readily affected by changes of temperature. Sometimes it is found advisable to thatch the roof, and in very hot weather to whitewash the tiles. Ample lighting and ventilation accommodation should be provided, the windows to face north, as direct sunlight in the hot weather is very injurious. The window frames must be fitted with fine-meshed wire gauze, to allow free ventilation without dust or flies.

For a well-equipped cheese-making dairy three rooms are necessary, namely, making-room or dairy and press room, ripening or cheese room, and scullery or place for washing up. With a large quantity of milk additional rooms are necessary, a store and separate press room.

The Dairy or Making-Room for a dairy of 50-60 cows should be 24 ft. × 15 ft. × 10 ft. high, but many dairies decidedly smaller than this may be quite con-

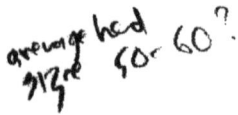

venient. The floor must be of some hard material impervious to moisture, portland cement, or concrete; if of the latter it must have a smooth surface; where flagstones or bricks are used they should be well cemented at the joints. The surface of the floor must be laid so as to slope towards an open gutter or surface drain, the drain running through an opening in the wall to a covered gully-trapped drain outside, and the whole so that it can be readily flushed and all taints thus prevented. Smooth plastered walls, having no crevices, which can be easily whitewashed, are the best, and if possible let the walls be tiled or cemented 4-5 ft. from the ground, so that they can be easily washed. The ceiling must also be plastered. Hot-water pipes running through assist in regulating the temperature, they are not absolutely essential, but are of great assistance where cheese is made all the year round. The supply of steam and of hot and cold water must be adequate to the amount of milk to be dealt with, the steam pipes fitted at a convenient place for the making vat or tub. The steam boiler, when part of the equipment, should be fixed near the making-room, possibly in the scullery, to prevent steam wastage.

A great deal of labor is saved and also dirt kept out of the dairy if there is some means for the milk to be poured into the cheese tub without the milkers coming into the dairy. A small receiver 18 in. square having a chute attached to it is good. The chute is passed through a small opening in the wall, or through the window of the dairy, to the cheese tub, the receiver being outside. The milk as soon as obtained is poured into the receiver covered with a coarse strainer cloth, and it then runs down the chute and before falling into the cheese vat, passes through a fine strainer cloth tied over the end. (See Plate A.)

Some method for conducting off the whey must be provided, either by removable gutters fitted from the top of the tub and running to an outside whey drain, or by means of a whey steam-lifter. (See Plate B.)

The whey runs from the tub into the pan e, and is sucked into the opening a, by the steam coming up the pipe b, which drives it up the pipe c, into the whey-lead d, or it may be driven directly to the mealhouse or piggeries, when not required for whey butter. These lifters are of great service where the fall is insufficient for the whey to run to the piggeries. The whey tank or whey-lead, as it is sometimes called, should be about 12 in. deep and of such a size as will hold the whey from one day's make of cheese. The pipe conducting the whey from the lead to the piggeries, should be made of glazed pipes, as whey soon perforates metal. The vessel for storing the whey when whey-butter is made, should, if possible, be always in a separate room outside the dairy. It is inadvisable to store utensils, etc., that are not in use, in the making-room, as the moisture from the steam, etc., tends to depreciate their value; therefore a shelf for just the necessary requirements and another for cloths, etc., are all that is wanted. A large making dairy is not advantageous, but there should be sufficient space for the vat or tub and curd cooler, and also room for presses and turning stool where there is not a separate press room. The presses must never be in a draught or cracked cheese will result. A small porcelain sink and draining table are of great value in a dairy, especially if the scullery is not close to the making-room.

THE SCULLERY may contain the steam boiler and copper, or furnace, but care must be taken that no smoke or dust can gain access to the dairy. In some dairies, the boiler is fixed in the making-room, but this is very undesirable, on account not only of the dirt, but also of the difficulty in cooling the dairy rapidly in hot weather. The copper must be of a size to provide an abundance of hot water, and there should be every convenience arranged in the scullery for the washing up of all dairy utensils.

RIPENING OR CURING ROOM can be either in the upper story, or on the same level. When above, attention should be paid that the ceiling, if close under the roof, is well packed with some non-conducting material (ex. sawdust). The windows must be covered with perforated zinc to

CHEDDAR CHEESE-MAKING.

prevent the intrusion of flies. A dry, well-ventilated atmosphere is desirable, the dryness being obtained by tubs of slaked lime; the temperature can be regulated by an arrangement with air bricks and hot-water pipes, or by the use of slow-combustion stoves. Hot-water or steam pipes, laid close to the walls, give the best means of heating, as all the sides of the cheese get an even temperature, a result not secured by stoves. Hot water retains heat longer than steam. If stoves are used, the floor should be damped occasionally or the atmosphere will be too dry.

In the best equipped dairies, the shelves for the cheese are those that can be turned together on an axle, as thus a great saving of labor is effected and there is less risk of damage to the cheese, but the cheese must be all of one size. Where ordinary shelves are used these should be made of $1\frac{1}{2}$ in. red deals, 18 in. wide, non-resinous wood and unpainted and with no knots, for these last harbor flies. They should be a good distance apart and have smooth edges, or in turning, the cheese may get cracked and broken and their market value lessened. Stands with removable shelves are convenient as they can be altered to the size of the cheese.

YEARLY PREPARATION OF THE DAIRY FOR CHEESE-MAKING.

Both the dairy and the cheese room should be thoroughly well lime-washed, the wash being made of two-thirds white lime and one-third cement, containing no size, as this attracts flies. It must be used in a fairly liquid state so that it reaches all crevices and cracks. If all woodwork is painted some color that shows splashes and spots, it is more likely to be kept clean; the paint can be cleaned occasionally with a good non-odoros disinfectant and soap, then should any insects or flies have deposited eggs, they are destroyed before the hot weather comes to give them a chance to develop into a plague.

The shelves and the floor in the cheese room, after being well scrubbed, should be well washed over with a weak solution of formalin. This may be bought at any chemist's, of the same strength as is used for disinfecting schools. The formalin destroys moulds and to a great extent prevents mites and flies, and if the operation is repeated during the season as each lot of cheese is sold and there is a clear space, much trouble is avoided. The floors of dairies by the end of a season sometimes begin to crack, it is therefore advisable before starting cheese-making to have them well cemented, so that there is no risk of stale whey collecting. If stones or cement become greasy, they can be cleaned with a pailful of scalding water containing about an eggcupful of sulphuric acid. The solution should be well brushed over, and the stones then rinsed down with clean hot water and the grease will be removed and the color of the stones lightened.

APPLIANCES FOR CHEDDAR CHEESE-MAKING.

The dairy where cheese-making is to be carried on must be well equipped. Good cheese can be made with make-shift utensils, but if a maker knows what is the best article, he is better able to adapt the article he has to use.

The following is a description of appliances of the most assistance as regards labor saving, an important item at the present time. Under existing circumstances it is difficult to give accurate prices, but those given are as near as the constant variation allows.

One of the first items in equipping a dairy is to provide for a regular supply of hot water. In small dairies a copper is found sufficient, but where more milk is dealt with it is a great saving of time and labor to have a steam boiler or generator. There are two types of boilers in common use—vertical (see illustration) and horizontal. The latter is usually bricked in and takes up rather more space, also it is usually more difficult to get at the interior of it when necessary to clean the rock or corroded substance, caused by hard water, on the sides. The main point to observe in any boiler, is that it has a comparatively small fire space, and that the heat from the fire comes in direct contact with the water tubes. The power of the boiler may be calculated by the grate area, roughly 1 sq. ft. of grate area equals 4 h.p., every 1 lb. coal evaporates 8 lb. water per hour, and every sq. ft. of grate will evaporate 120 lb. water per hour.

It is of the greatest importance that there should be an easily adjusted safety plug, in case the water should be low in the boiler, the plug will melt out, and the remainder of the water will put out the fire and no damage is done to

STEAM BOILER.

the boiler, a new plug can be refixed without the delay of fetching a mechanic for the purpose. In the vertical boiler, this is easily done by opening the front and screwing the plug in inside. These boilers (48 in. × 20 in. diam., 1¼ h.p.) are suitable for a dairy dealing with 100-150 gallons of milk daily, and cost about £23 10s. complete with fittings. With the smaller quantity of milk, this would also provide sufficient steam for driving off the whey to the piggeries, if at no great distance. They are very economical in fuel, and except when steam is required quickly, will burn almost any rubbish, if the flues are regularly cleaned once a week. The value of a boiler is enhanced according to its position; when fixed close to the dairy no steam is wasted, and the best results are obtained. Too much importance cannot be given to the method for supplying the boiler with water. Where water from the main supply is used, the pressure is usually sufficient to allow of the boiler being filled when steam is low, but where it is necessary to pump the water into the boiler, a great deal of anxiety is saved, if there are two separate means—i.e., a hand or donkey-pump and a steam injector. Thus, if one gets out of order, there is always another to fall back upon. The main points in working a boiler are as follows:—Before lighting the fire see that the glass-gauge is in working order by opening the taps. Note the height of the water and if necessary pump in a fresh supply. Having lighted the fire, as soon as steam is up, see that on blowing the water from the gauge-glass, it refills immediately on closing the cock, showing that the passages have not been even partially closed by any sediment from the water which collects there. To make certain that this is all right, the top cock on the gauge must always be open. Next see that the steam valve is in working order, lift the weight slightly and blow off, noting if the gauge pressure corresponds. All steam taps connected with the boiler must be turned off after use, as often when the boiler cools, a vacuum is caused in it and the water will be sucked back from the copper, where the steam valve may have been turned in to use up the last lot of steam. If possible, always use soft water for the boiler, many people collect the condensed steam, as it does not make it necessary to clean the boilers so often.

The chimney from a steam generator should be wide and high, to take away the soot, otherwise it will fall and contaminate surroundings.

CHEDDAR CHEESE-MAKING. 15

CHEESE VATS AND TUBS.

There are two types of vessels in use for the actual making of the cheese, namely the oblong jacketed vat, and the round tin or copper tub, which is sometimes steam-jacketed, and occasionally has a jacket for water, or more commonly has no means of retaining heat at all.

OBLONG JACKETED VATS are the newer type and are gradually becoming more common as they are better

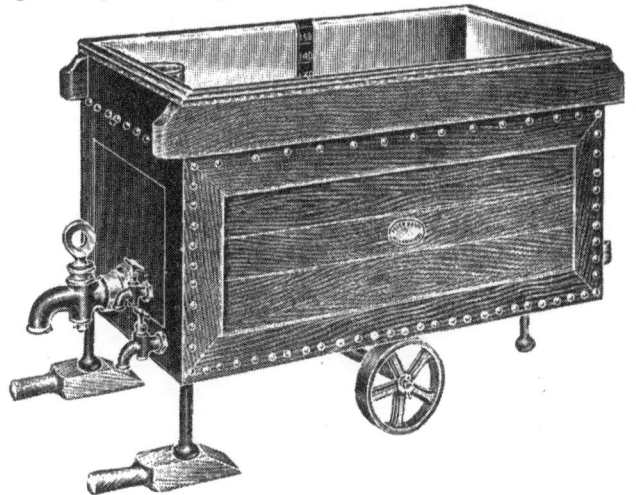

OBLONG JACKETED VAT.

known. They are easier to work (especially with large quantities) during the whole process of manufacture, particularly in cutting the curd, and drawing off the whey, and they provide an excellent means of cooling the evening's milk without the trouble of pouring it over a refrigerator. Added to this, they can be used for the entire process of cheese-making, the curd remaining in the vat on racks instead of being taken to the cooler. Warm water can be put in the jacket to help on the cheese in cold weather, and cold water to retard the working in the hot weather, thus the additional cost of a cooler is saved. They can be obtained in any capacity from 40-600 gallons and cost for 100 gallons £15 10s.; for 250 gallons £23. The outer packet is of strong sheet iron, painted to resemble wood, the inner of well tinned metal, in some cases tinned copper. The inside is made smaller than the jacket, leaving a space of about 2 in. for water at the bottom and up the sides of the vessel. It is set upon three legs with two wheels in the middle. The two front legs are made short and are wedged up, with blocks when the vat is in use, to draw off the whey the blocks can be removed and the vat tilted, the whey drains away readily. The tap is fitted inside with a sieve to prevent pieces of curd from escaping. The vat should have a gauge to show the quantity of milk. If not, the capacity can be estimated by measuring the vat, each cubic foot will hold $6\frac{1}{4}$ gallons.

The steam comes into the jacket, by means of pipes entering from the back and lying on the bottom of the jacket running lengthways, S. In some vats, these pipes are perforated so that the steam heats the water regularly all over the bottom. There is an inlet for water also at the back, and two taps to draw off the waste water are in front. A large tap is fixed through the jacket into the vat for running off the whey, etc. If this tap and the two water taps are unscrewed, and the three screws which fix it at the back end are removed, the whole of the inner jacket can be lifted out. This should be done every year, and the lining painted with non-odorous red lead to keep the vessel in good repair and prevent rusting during the winter months. All steam valves must fit well or the curd at one part will become harder than at another.

ROUND CHEESE TUBS NOT JACKETED.—These should be of well tinned metal, preferably tinned copper, having as few seams as possible, and should stand on a solid wood stand fitted with a lever for tilting when drawing off the whey. Price without stand for 60 gallons, £3 10s.; 100 gallons, £5 2s. 6d.

PLATE A.—DAIRY, SHOWING MILK COMING INTO VAT BY CHUTE.

(See page 9)

PLATE B.—STEAM WHEY-LIFTER.

(See page 9)

CHEDDAR CHEESE-MAKING. 17

ROUND TIN TUB.

JACKETED TUB.

JACKETED CHEESE TUB.—Made with copper inside pan and tinned-steel jacket or made from all copper. The steam in the jacket should run in water and not come in direct contact with the sides of the tub, as this is liable to cook the curd to the sides of the vessel. If the pipes be in water there is no danger of burning the curd with the heat coming from the bottom, as well as the sides of the tub. These can be had in any size. If not fitted with a gauge, the capacity may be estimated by measuring the diameter and multiplying it by itself, deduct $\frac{1}{5}$; the result multiplied by the depth and by $6\frac{1}{4}$ will give the capacity.

OVERHEAD HEATER OR WARMER.—At one time there was a prejudice against steam-jacketed tubs owing to their misuse when first introduced. Cheese-makers

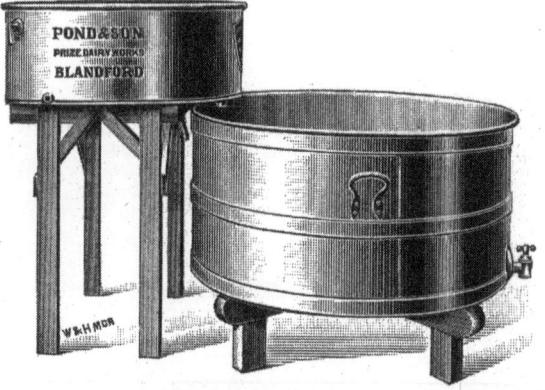

OVERHEAD HEATER.

appeared to think the steam would make the cheese and neglected to keep the curd well stirred and it became clotted and matted on the bottom of the tub. An additional steam-heated vessel was then introduced in which the milk and whey are warmed. This entails more work, as in addition to the labor of dipping the milk and whey into it for heating, it is an extra and difficult article to clean. The great point in its favor is that the heater may be used with any size tub, according to the time of the year.

CURD COOLER.

These may be of tin only or of wood with a well-tinned lining (as illustration) fitted with either tin, iron,

CURD COOLER.

or wooden racks and a plug hole for whey or water. The prices vary according to size from £3 to £7 with stand.

CURD KNIVES.

THE AMERICAN CURD KNIVES give decidedly better results than any other method of cutting. There is less loss of fat and curd, the cutting is regular without smashing. They consist of thin strips of tinned steel soldered together. The pair cost from £2 10s. to £2 15s. according to size.

POND'S DIAGONAL KNIFE costs rather less than the pair

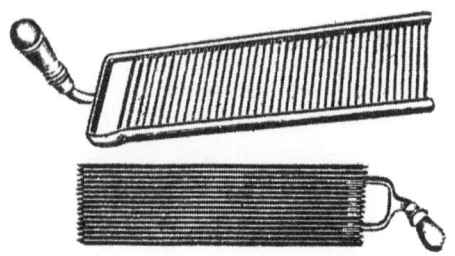

AMERICAN CURD KNIVES.

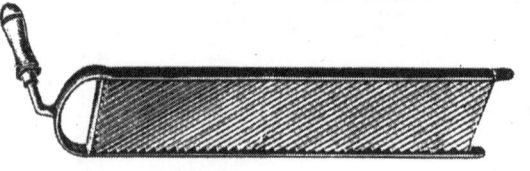

POND'S CURD KNIFE.

of American knives 35s., and gives very good results, the curd is cut into diamond-shaped pieces.

CURD-BREAKER AND STIRRER.—The breaker is more useful for stirring the curd in a round tub, than for breaking it, as it is liable to smash the curd and waste fat, etc. It is important, if used for cutting, that the wire and edges are sharp. The old idea was to have a blunt breaker, it was thought that the curd would then break where there was most moisture, but in practice it is found that the curd is more inclined to smash than break.

CURD BREAKER.

CURD RAKE.—This resembles a hay rake, except that

the teeth are on either side of the blade, which is set at right angles to a long handle. It is made of light wood and is used for stirring the curd in the oblong vats. It

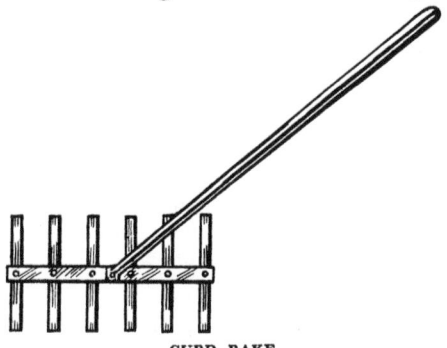

CURD RAKE.

can usually be made locally, costing from 5s. to 10s. In factories mechanical agitators are used for stirring the curd, they are fitted with cone-pulleys, so that the speed can be regulated according to the condition of the curd.

MILK STRAINER.—A sieve of fine mesh, fitted with hooks, to hang on to cheese vat or tub made with a flat side for the former. It removes the larger particles

MILK STRAINER.

MILK BOWL.

of dirt before the milk passes through the cloth tied on the outside of the strainer. Cost 9s. to 12s. each.

TIN MILK BOWL.—For stirring in the rennet, etc. Must have a sound handle, or sour milk will collect in it. Price, 2s. 9d. to 3s. 3d.

CURD MILL.—These may be had either to fit on to the cooler or cheese vat, or on an iron stand, with removable box for weighing and emptying the curd, the whole is on wheels so that it can be moved about on the front runners.

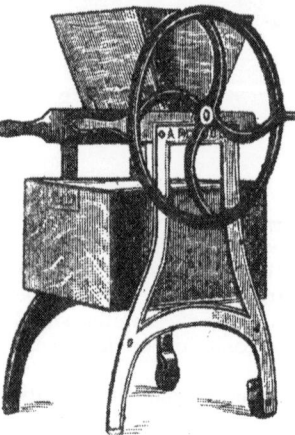

CURD MILL.

The chute may be of either wood or metal (the latter preferable as it is easier to keep clean). The inside consists of a roller with rounded and blunt spokes, and metal grating. The spokes on the roller pass through the opening in the grating, tearing the curd into pieces, the curd then falls through into the box underneath. The whole is fitted to a cast-iron frame.

The chief points of a good curd mill are that the spokes shall not be sharp and that the curd is torn apart and passed through without squeezing out the fat.

Old-fashioned mills which grind the curd very finely, and tend to pulverize it, may be improved by removing one or two bars of the metal grating, the curd passes through more rapidly without being torn so fine. Curd mills with double rollers are not desirable for cheddar cheese, as they break the curd too finely and are much heavier to turn than an ordinary single-roller. Price to fix on cooler, £2 10s.; with fly-wheel, £3 12s. 6d.; on stand with box, £4—£4 10s.

CHEDDAR CHEESE-MAKING. 23

CURD SIEVE.—To catch curd when drawing off whey, brass wire is preferable, as easier to keep clean than the ordinary hair sieves. Price, 3s. 6d. to 4s. 6d.

CURD SCOOP.—For filling the moulds or vats with

CURD SIEVE.

CURD WHISK.

CURD SCOOP.

curd, work can be done more speedily than with plates, etc. Cost, 3s. 6d. to 4s. 6d.

CURD WHISK.—This facilitates the removal of the curd

TRUCKLE MOULD.

CHEDDAR MOULD.

24 CHEDDAR CHEESE-MAKING.

when drawing off the whey and is also of great assistance at vatting. Price, 1s. 3d. to 1s. 6d.

TRUCKLE VATS OR MOULDS.—Made in varying sizes, to make 8 lb. to 18 lb. cheese. The most common, 11 in. × 6½ in., 9s. 6d. each with followers, two tin and one wooden. They can also be had with handles.

CHEDDAR VATS OR MOULDS.—Made of strong tinned metal having perforated holes for the whey to drain off and closely-fitting tin followers and lid. The latter are made of strong wood with bars across to facilitate removal. Price, per set of three : 13 in. diam., £3 13s. 6d. ; 14 in diam., £3 16s 6d. ; 14½ in. diam., £4 ; 15 in. diam., £4

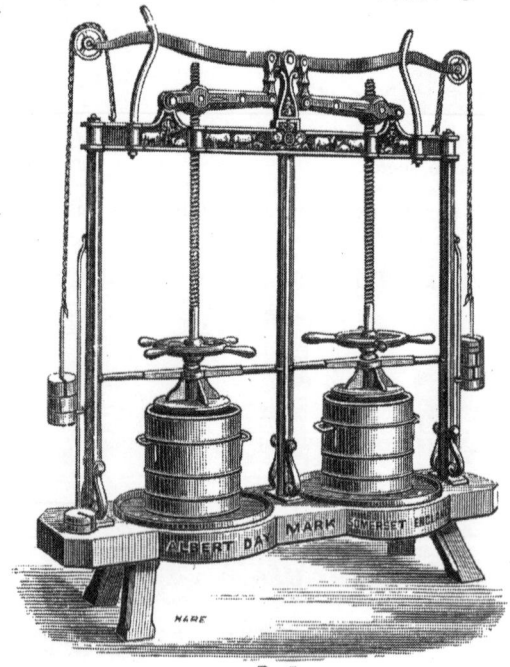

DOUBLE CHEESE PRESS.

CHEESE PRESSES.

There are two types of the ordinary upright cheese press in common use; worked by bar and chain lever; in addition to these there is another type of upright press, where the pressure is regulated by a strong spring acting on the screw, the amount used being shown on a small scale.

DOUBLE PRESS WITH CHAIN AND LEVER (1).—This press, in addition to the pressure obtained by leverage, has a chain fixed to the stand which passes over the wheel at the end of the long lever, and the weights are hung on the end of the chain instead of the lever. This contrivance doubles the pressure without using exceptionally heavy weights, or long levers.

SINGLE PRESS WITH LEVER ONLY (2).—With this type of press, a longer bar for leverage or heavier weights must be used, to cause the same pressure on the cheese as obtained with the above.

SINGLE CHEESE PRESS.

Both types of press are usually weighed to press up to 1½ tons pressure when all weights are on, counting the screw pressure as well.

The presses are made of strong metal, great pressure being obtained in a small space. The screw, when tightened on to the cheese, on the platform, lifts the lever, upon which the weights are put to decrease or increase weight on the cheese.

TO CALCULATE PRESSURE ON THE CHEESE.

1. TYPE OF PRESS.—The weight hanging on the end of the chain at *a* is doubled at *b* by the force exerted at *c*. Multiply the weight at *b* by the total length of the bar *d*, and divide by the small lever *e*, this will give the force exerted at *f*. Multiply this figure by the length *g*, and divide by the small lever *h*, this will give the pressure on the screw *i*. The weight of the screw added to this will give the weight on the cheese *j*.

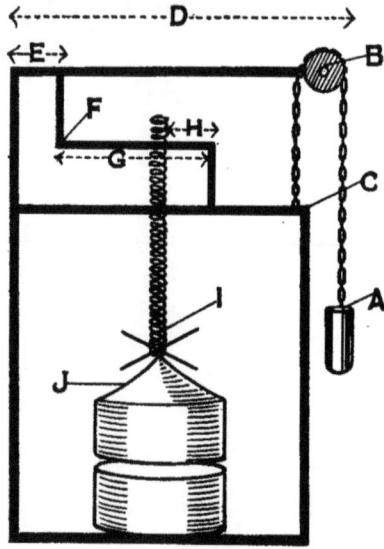

DIAGRAM OF CHEESE PRESS.

The pressure on the second type of press is calculated as for the above, except that the direct weight put on is taken at the end of the long bar.

GANG CHEESE PRESS.—Where a number of cheese have to be pressed a horizontal gang press is used; the cheese are placed on their sides and pressure applied with a screw and powerful lever. The gang press is so fitted that constant pressure is maintained while the cheese is in the press. It requires less room and is especially valuable where a large quantity of milk is dealt with.

CHEESE STOOL.—For turning the cheese on during the time they are pressing. This stool must be, if possible, the centre cutting from strong oak or elm, as the bumping out of the cheese soon causes the wood to splinter.

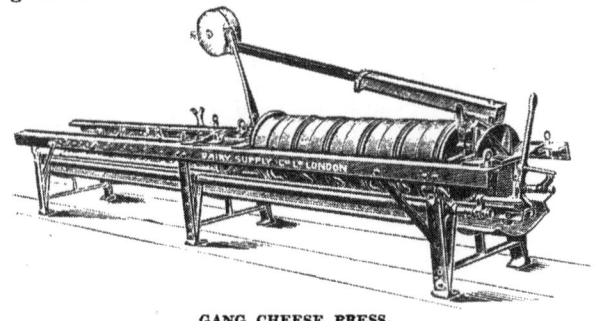

GANG CHEESE PRESS.

Set on four stout legs, and of such a height as is convenient to handle the cheese.

OTHER APPLIANCES that may be mentioned as of importance in a cheese-making factory are:—

1. STEAMING-BLOCK OR STAND, for pails and churns, a great preventive of taints, as live steam is the best method of destroying injurious organisms.

2. REFRIGERATOR OR COOLER to cool evening's milk, where no jacketed vat or tub is available.

3. WEIGHING MACHINE for the curd and cheese.

4. PORTABLE STOVE for fixing in cheese-room where there are no steam or hot-water pipes.

5. DAIRY SCALES for weighing salt, etc.

6. SALT BOX made of well seasoned wood that will not taint the salt and will keep it dry.

AMONG THE SMALLER REQUIREMENTS of the dairy too much importance cannot be given to the thermometers in use. They should be glass and floating thermometers; with a scale and thread of mercury, that can be easily read. The same kind can be used for making the cheese and for hanging in the dairy, and should register up to boiling point. Thermometers must be correct, they require to be tested periodically with a registered thermometer, as occasionally the paper scale slips. Price 2s. 6d.

A detailed description of the smaller apparatus required for testing the acidity of milk is given in Chapter IV. The cost of the acidimeter complete with solutions is £1 2s. 6d. The measure glass and pipette for the rennet test can be obtained for 3s. 6d. to 4s. 6d. and the 'Hot Iron,' if made locally from a bar of iron, put into a handle, costs from 8d. to 1s.

As REGARDS MATERIALS, the price is constantly changing. The cheapest quality flannelette is best for strainer cloth and now costs $4\frac{1}{4}d.$ to $4\frac{3}{4}d.$ per yd. A material known as the hygienic strainer cloth can be bought in some districts for $10\frac{1}{2}d.$ per yd.

CHEESE-GREY.—The thinner quality for underbands costs $3\frac{3}{4}d.$ to $4\frac{1}{4}d.$ per yd., the stouter for rack cloths $4\frac{1}{4}d.$ to $4\frac{3}{4}d.$ Coarse cheese cloth for rack cloths $11\frac{1}{2}d.$ per yd. Unbleached calico for outside or roller bands $4\frac{1}{2}d.$ to $5\frac{1}{2}d.$ per yd. Stout banding material for outside bands, according to width $8\frac{1}{2}d.$ to 1s. $3\frac{1}{2}d.$

CHAPTER IV.

SKILL OF MAKER. THE CONTROL OF ACIDITY AND MOISTURE. ACIDITY TESTS. USE OF STARTER.

SKILL OF MAKER.

For the production of a uniform, commercial cheese under varying conditions, great skill is required on the part of the maker. Given the best conditions, namely good pure milk, convenient dairy and appliances, and a satisfactory method, an inexperienced cheese-maker can turn out a marketable article.

Where conditions are poor, soils variable, milk tainted and utensils indifferent, the utmost skill is required to battle with defects. People taking a sufficient interest in their subject can become skilled, but they must as each adverse occasion arises, go to the root of the matter, and never rest until the cause has been found and a further occurrence prevented. In this way, valuable information is found, and the maker is better able to tackle other problems as they occur. A successful cheese-maker must be quick to think and to act. He must know his work and be able to apply his knowledge to control variations caused by climatic and local agents. He should work with an ideal in view and never rest until this result has been obtained.

THE CONTROL OF ACIDITY AND MOISTURE.

Acidity and moisture with Temperature, are the main factors in the production of all varieties of cheese. When a maker has once acquired the knowledge of when and how to control the acidity and moisture, half the actual difficulties in cheese-making are overcome.

Before the introduction of starters the process could only be hastened by a rise in temperature, and the main difficulties of a cheese-maker were, in the cool weather to get the cheese to work quick enough and in hot weather to check the development of acidity. Excessive moisture unduly hastens acidity and the curd works too rapidly, therefore to check it, the curd is dried by cutting scalding or by pressure in various ways. When the acidity is low, moisture is kept in the curd as much as possible to hasten development, but no exact rule can be laid down with regard to the amount of moisture at different stages. This has to be determined by the nature of the district and soil from which the milk is obtained. (See effect of soil on cheese-making Chapter II.) The degree of acidity which the milk reaches at fixed times must be accurately gauged, formerly it was entirely a matter of individual judgment based on the taste, smell and appearance of the curd. The rough but approximate guess so obtained is no longer satisfactory with the demand for a uniform marketable cheese and greater accuracy can be obtained by the use of tests; tests have the further advantage that they can be used by people whose experience is not great and whose judgment is unsound.

MOISTURE IN THE CURD.—Moisture is required for the proper development of acidity to control the ripening and to give flavor and mellowness to the finished cheese. The amount of moisture in the curd is affected by many outside influences, thus curds from sweet or over-ripe milk, retain a larger proportion of moisture than those from medium milk. A high temperature at renneting and a low proportion of rennet, with a normal renneting temperature tends to cause a moist curd, and a remarkable difference is shown when the curd is cut into different sizes. Thus comparing a cheddar curd ($\frac{1}{4}$ in. cubes) with a Derby ($\frac{3}{4}$ in. cubes) there is nearly half as much again moisture in the latter, as in the former.

If the scalding process is carried out too rapidly the outside of the curd becomes cooked or hardened while the inside remains moist, later when the moisture from this softer curd is expelled, there is loss in yield. Therefore curd from over-ripe milk which tends to hold moisture, should be cut fine and scalded slowly to get rid of all superfluous moisture. Thick piling of the curd on the rack increases the moisture content, therefore to get rid of any excess the curd should be kept well stirred to prevent matting and should not be put to press until dry. Extra salt also dries the curd. An excess of moisture in cheese not only causes too high acidity but the cheese is liable to leak, lose flavor rapidly and eventually become bitter through excessive fermentation.

The fact that milk previous to renneting contains a larger percentage of acidity than does the whey from the curd immediately after cutting has led to much discussion and at the present time there is a difference of opinion as to the cause. Some say that the casein, an acid substance in semi-solution, is thrown out of solution by the rennet in coagulation and becomes insoluble, thus the whey is sweeter. Others give the opinion that the action of rennet on milk tends to liberate some of the lime-salts, thus rendering them soluble, these soluble lime-salts then neutralize some of the acidity in the whey. A yet further opinion is that some of the acidity in milk is due to the presence of carbon dioxide which is given off during the process, there is no doubt that this phenomenon is very difficult for either the student or the practical farmhouse cheese-maker to understand and causes the latter in some cases a great deal of anxiety when first using the acidimeter.

TESTS FOR ACIDITY IN CHEESE-MAKING.—Some reliable and accurate test for acidity must be used if a maker is to turn out a uniform lot of cheese, for judgment can only be obtained after years of experience and then perhaps only one person in every hundred is especially gifted in this direction.

The three most common tests in use are: The Acidimeter, Rennet Test, and Hot-Iron Test.

THE ACIDIMETER.—In this test, the acidity in the milk is neutralized by a standard solution of caustic soda and an indicator (phenol phthalein) used, which turns pink as soon as the acid solution of milk or whey becomes alkaline with the caustic soda. The quantities taken are measured and the percentage of acidity calculated from this.

APPARATUS REQUIRED.—A 25 cubic centimetre burette graduated to measure 1/10th of a cubic centimetre is fixed to a stand. It is filled with the standard solution up to the 0 mark. The solution is of such a strength that 1 c.c. of it will neutralize .01% of a gram of lactic acid in the 10 c.c. of milk taken for the test. A drop bottle is necessary for the indicator so that the 3 drops required can be measured accurately. A 10 c.c. pipette for measuring the liquid to be tested and a small dish in which to take the test and a glass stirring rod are required.

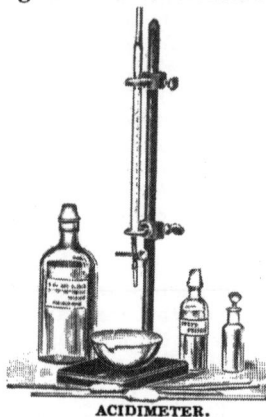

ACIDIMETER.

The test is taken as follows: Measure 10 c.c. of the milk or whey and run into the dish, add 3 drops of the indicator phenol phthalein. Slowly add the solution from the burette to the liquid in the dish, stirring meanwhile. As it mixes with the sample a pink color appears but if stirred this will disappear. The solution is added gradually until a faint permanent pink color is obtained and the quantity used is then read off from the burette. If 2 c.c. have been used then $.01 \times 2$ grams is the amount of lactic acid present in the 10 c.c. taken. Thus in 100 c.c. there would be 10 times this amount, that is $.01 \times 2 \times 10$, the result .2% lactic acid present. In practice it simplifies matters to merely move the decimal place backward and the number then represents the percentage of acidity present in the milk. The advantages are that it can be used at all stages in cheese-making namely (1) before renneting (2) before drawing off the whey (3) to test the drawings from the cooler and the press.

PLATE C.—CURD IN TUB AFTER DRAWING OFF WHEY.

(*See page* 49)

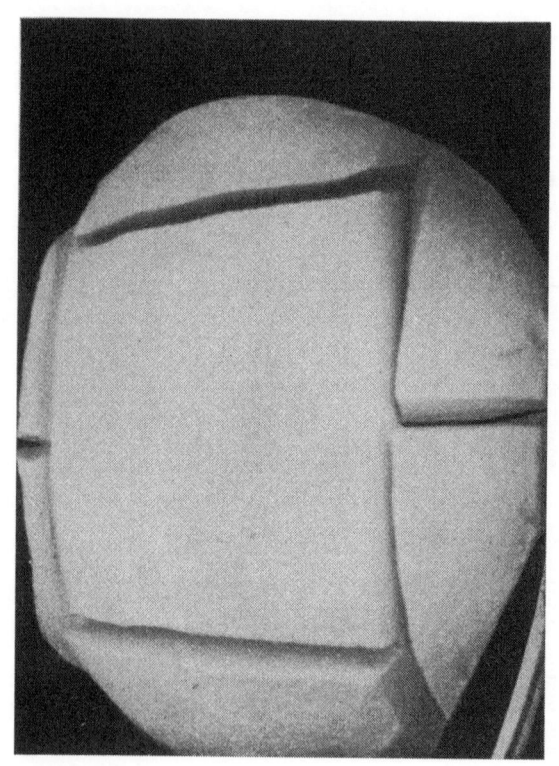

PLATE D.—CURD CUT FOR PILING IN TUB.

(See page 49)

CHEDDAR CHEESE-MAKING.

According to some authorities it is not so useful to the cheese-maker as the rennet test, as during the so-called 'period of incubation' of the milk i.e. the time before renneting, the number of bacteria present may be increased many thousandfold, but the acidity registered remains stationary. There are occasions on record when it has not shown the presence of acidity, when according to other tests the milk and curd have been sufficiently acid at the various stages. Sometimes too when the curd has been good and free from taints, the tests taken of the whey drawings from the press will show less acidity than before grinding. These are both cases where further knowledge is required to obtain adequate information of the cause of such uncommon circumstances. Possibly the failure of the test is due to some abnormal condition of the milk affected by the presence of a greater or less amount of lime-salts, as it has been found that the more acidity in the curd, the larger the proportion of lime will come off in the whey.

THE RENNET TEST.—This is a simple and inexpensive test requiring great accuracy in working and then small differences in acidity can be readily detected by it.

UTENSILS REQUIRED.—4 oz. measure glass, 5 c.c. pipette graduated to 1/10 of a c.c., a cup, and a few pieces of straw, a stop watch or a clock with a second hand.

Four ounces of the mixed milk for renneting at 84° F. are measured in the glass and into the cup 3.55 or 1 dram of rennet is put with two or three pieces of straw. The cup should be slightly warm to prevent the lowering of the temperature of the milk. The watch or clock is placed near the cup and the exact time noted when the milk is poured on to the rennet. This is stirred with the thermometer for 15 seconds and when the thermometer is removed the temperature is noted, one degree either above or below will make a difference of two seconds in the test. When the milk begins to coagulate, the straws will stop moving and the time must be taken. The number of seconds from the time of adding the milk to the rennet, to when the straws stop moving, gives the test. In comparison with the acidimeter the rennet test is as follows :—

.20% lactic acid by acidimeter corresponds to 24 seconds rennet test.

.21% lactic acid by acidimeter corresponds to 21 or 22 seconds rennet test.

.22% lactic acid by acidimeter corresponds to 20 seconds rennet test.

.24% lactic acid by acidimeter corresponds to 18 seconds rennet test.

This is a very reliable test but the rennet used must be of standard strength and great care should be taken to have the temperature accurate.

HOT IRON TEST.—A smooth flat bar of iron, about 1 in. wide and ¼ in. thick, fitted into a handle is required. It is heated to a 'black heat' and when the surface has been cleaned on a brick, a piece of curd previously squeezed dry is rubbed on the iron and then drawn carefully away. Silky threads attach themselves to the iron and their length denotes the acidity present. Acidity has the effect of partially digesting the casein of the curd so that it will 'draw' when heated and the length and fineness of the threads before they break from the curd are reliable indications of acidity. ¼ in. threads are equal to .18-.19% lactic acid on the acidimeter 1½ in.-1¾ in. =.8-.9%. When the acidity is above 1% the curd will not draw but simply melts on the iron. If the iron is not hot enough the curd will not stick, and if too hot it will become blackened. It is a test of great service in practical cheese-making as it is more easily worked than a chemical test and is simpler to the lay mind. It is viewed with great contempt by some chemists as there seems no adequate reason for it, but cheese of good uniform make is turned out where it is the only test used. If the rennet test is employed before renneting and the hot iron when drawing off the whey and before grinding the curd, very good results can be obtained.

THE USE OF STARTER IN CHEESE-MAKING.

In the manufacture of all hard-pressed varieties of cheese a certain amount of acidity is necessary before renneting, it can be produced in two ways, either by mixing the ripened evening's milk with the morning's, or by ripening the bulk of milk in the morning before renneting. The ripening or souring of the milk may be brought about in two ways, either allow it to sour naturally, assisting it by keeping it warm, or add a pure culture starter. The original method was to ripen the evening's milk sufficiently by keeping it covered in the tub over night, and in some cases even warming it so that when the morning's milk was added enough acidity was present. The results are good where the milk is obtained under the cleanest possible conditions and where there is no great variation in temperature during the evening, as the natural organisms in the milk are of the kind favorable to cheese-making and it is their development that is required. But where there is a likelihood of uncleanliness, the injurious organisms containable in milk increase rapidly during the night at the high temperature, and cause the whole of the next day's milk to be tainted. Originally anything that was added to the milk to hasten souring was termed a starter, and sour milk and whey were and are still used for the purpose. These when good, give good results but should one day's milk or cheese be tainted the following day's will be spoilt by the addition of the tainted sour milk or whey. The introduction of pure culture starters into cheese-making has to a great extent done away with an enormous quantity of tainted cheese, and at the same time produces a uniform article. The starter consists of milk in which are growing lactic acid bacteria in as near a pure state as is possible under the circumstances. These organisms are found in the atmosphere or in naturally soured milk, but when grown in a purer form they are more vigorous and are able to overcome any injurious organisms that may be present in the milk to which they are added. All organisms increase rapidly at a high temperature, namely 70°-90° F., and for this reason milk sours rapidly

21°-32° C

in warm weather. Therefore if the evening's milk on a farm is cooled as soon as obtained down to 70° F. the growth of any organisms in it is checked. Next morning on adding a certain quantity of a pure culture starter, these organisms have full play and ripen the milk with a pure acidity. The proper use of the starter resembles the preparation of the soil and the freeing it from weeds, previous to the sowing of good seed.

[21°C]

Starters when first employed were much abused, many cheese-makers adding a large quantity without judgment, with the consequence that over-acid cheese was produced and starters fell in bad repute. For the successful use a moderate quantity should be added to the milk some time (1½-2 hours) before rennetting. In this way the milk is ripened gradually, the organisms become acclimatized and are better able to act in the later stages of the curd, producing a mellowness and silkiness that are never otherwise attained. The quantity required varies usually ¼-1% according to the district, but it can be ascertained by the fact that the cheese should be ready to vat 7-8 hours after adding the starter.

[RENNET TO MILL 5-6½ HRS]

PREPARATION OF THE STARTER FOR HOME USE.

Starters should only be prepared by experts from whom they can be obtained by the ordinary cheese-maker, as they are in a form easily used. A bottle of starter may be obtained from any of the various Dairy Schools and Colleges and with this quantity sufficient must be made for the next day's use. The amount will vary according to the quantity of cheese being made.

Procure a well-enamelled jug or milk-can; the latter is usually more convenient as it can easily be suspended in a copper or furnace. Thoroughly scald the vessel and measure in some well strained milk that is sweet, fresh and free from all objectionable tastes and odors. Milk that has been through a separator is preferable as all dirt has been driven out of it by centrifuging; but this is not always to be had. The vessel should then be placed in hot water and the temperature raised quickly to 185° F.,

[85°C]

left for 10 minutes and cooled quickly to 65° F. in summer and 75° F. in winter, care must be taken that it is in a pure atmosphere. Then add the starter from the bottle and mix well. Cover with a clean cloth that will not allow any particles of dirt to pass through and keep at an even temperature until next day. In winter it must not be allowed to become too cold but care must be taken that it is not too warm, or a hard curd is formed, the organisms use up all the available food in the milk and are not so active later when put into the milk for cheese-making. Should they produce too much acidity they eventually destroy themselves, hence the reason for making a fresh starter daily, and it is of no use to reserve any of the contents of the bottle for future use.

A good starter should be in a soft, curdy mass when ready for use and when stirred should have a creamy appearance, not slimy, curdy, or watery, it should be free from frothiness, or gasiness, with a clean acid taste and aroma, showing .65-.75% lactic acid on the acidimeter and strong and vigorous in producing acidity when added to the milk for cheese-making.

Before adding .the starter to the milk about $\frac{1}{2}$ pint should be reserved to make the starter for the next day; this is instead of the bottleful of bought culture.

When the starter shows signs of weakness, that is if the cheese works slowly several days following, or has a bad flavor or odor a fresh culture should be obtained. Under unsuitable conditions a really good starter may become quite unfit for use in a few days, but if propagated daily under suitable conditions may remain practically pure for months.

A starter ought to be a starter only, and in its literal sense should be used to start the ripening on the proper lines.

CHAPTER V

THE MAKING OF CHEDDAR CHEESE.

CHEDDAR cheese may be said to be the chief variety of hard or pressed cheese. It is the most easily adaptable method of cheese-making for the milk from various soils and districts, and therefore has a wider market than any other kind.

Although at the present time, there are two main districts of manufacture in Great Britain, i.e. Somerset and South Western Scotland, yet it must be borne in mind that the method in the latter district was adapted from the former to suit the new locality. Cheddar has been made in Scotland only during the last sixty or seventy years, but such attention has been given to the process that in competition with the Somerset makers the Scotch often come out victorious.

From the small village of Cheddar where this system of cheese-making took its name, the method has spread and forged far ahead of its starting-point. Thus we find large co-operative cheese factories in America and in Australia, New Zealand and other parts of the British Empire, while in the original district it is still carried on in farmhouses, both under what may be termed primitive, as well as up-to-date methods. The factories in Somerset were started in the first place to deal with the surplus milk in the early summer season.

It is a lamentable fact that the class of cheese turned out is still anything but uniform, and the dairies where first-class cheese is made are in the minority. The greater part of the cheese produced must be termed second rate, and this description applies to nearly all the factory cheese that does not belong to an even lower class. This is sure to be the case until the public have a better idea of a high standard of cleanliness. It is useless to blame land, cows, systems of make or anything else if ordinary care is not taken that the milk is produced under hygienic conditions. We find the best cheese made in individual farmhouses, merely because these particular individuals themselves attend to the production of pure milk. Unless the farmer himself superintends the milking, and the cheese-maker herself attends to the cleansing of the utensils, etc., nothing is satisfactory. In these days few paid workers think of the final result of present uncleanliness.

The cause of inferior factory cheese is easily seen. The vendors of milk in many cases are thoroughly careless in the production of the same, as they are not troubled with the after results. The milk goes to many factories, unstrained, warm, and in vessels that have not been thoroughly cleansed. Many factories find it convenient to receive the milk once a day only. Consequently the milk stands about at the farm, possibly uncooled and often in an impure atmosphere, and so long as it is not actually sour it is thought to be immaterial. This milk on reaching the factory is mixed with pure milk and contaminates the whole.

Next at the factory, we find inadequate appliances for dealing with the large bulk that comes at some periods of the year. The labor in many cases is unskilled. The cheese-maker (often a man who has previously attended to the boiler and just gleaned scraps of information) has no idea of the elementary rules governing the control of milk for cheese-making. He will have hundreds of gallons of sour whey standing about which he dare not waste, first because of its money value and secondly owing to the injurious effect it has upon sewer-drains. This, when the whey tanks become full, is kept in any available vessel, and the milk for cheese-making stands every chance of becoming tainted.

The store where the cheese is ripened in many cases is too susceptible to changes of temperature. Heat in summer causes the cheese to leak and therefore to become dry and rancid when ready for sale. Sometimes the store is in close proximity to the boiler-house, which makes it impossible to lower the temperature in hot weather.

In the making of cheddar cheese of a uniform quality

a great many agencies are concerned. Prime cheese can be made by quite inexperienced cheese-makers, when conditions are favorable. But when a difficult season comes, change of land or adverse conditions, skill and experience are absolutely necessary to turn out an even and regular lot of cheese. If we compare the earlier and later systems the first great difference we notice is the hastening of the whole process. The object is to produce a uniform article in a definite time with as little labor as possible. In olden days cheese-making continued through the day from early morning till late evening, some people having to wait up at night to vat their cheese. At the present, 6 to 8 hours is found sufficient time for the process of bringing about a mellowed cheese. Formerly the maker was entirely dependent on outside temperature for the production of acidity and this was difficult to obtain in cold weather. It is for this reason that the introduction of starters has to such a great extent given the maker control over the process. The production of and control of acidity is the main point of cheddar cheese making, both in the milk before renneting and in the curd during the later stages. It assists the action of the rennet in the contraction of the curd to get rid of the moisture and also produces those mellow and elastic properties desirable for a typical cheddar curd. It partially digests the casein, which change brings about the mellowing of the curd. Where a starter is not used the maker is dependent on the action of bacteria which have gained access to the milk naturally; well and good, if the milk has been obtained in the cleanest possible way, the ripening or souring, although usually slower than when a starter is added, will be entirely satisfactory. But, should the milk contain injurious organisms, their growth will be encouraged by the warmth necessary during the night for the ripening of the evening's milk, and by the addition of such milk to the bulk in the morning, the cheese stands every chance of becoming tainted.

It was the misuse of starter when it was first introduced that brought it in bad repute with first-class cheese-makers. The starter in the hands of careless people, who expected it to cover any dirt, was used in such large

Scotch
Candy
Cannon

Cheddar Cheese-making.

quantities that hard dry cheese was the result. Individual makers learn from experience to use the smallest quantity, and they gradually find the amount suitable to their own particular milk.

The presence of the pure lactic acid bacteria ensures to a great extent a good flavor in the finished article, for the bacteria overcomes undesirable organisms, which might produce bitterness, etc. Acidity is also necessary for the digestive action of the ferments during the ripening of the cheese.

There are many systems of cheddar cheese making in vogue. Individuals, working on a definite system, vary their method according to the requirements of the milk they are using, and the best maker in each case can and does turn out a first-class article.

It is proposed to give a brief comparison of some of the commoner systems, and to show how they all have the same end in view; in addition, to give a method which the writer has found by experience both with large and small quantities of milk and on many different soils, to be the least laborious; and at the same time to produce a cheese that is appreciated by dealers, whether from Somerset, the Midlands, Scotland or London. The Scotch, Candy's and Cannon's methods are quite distinct. In the following description, it is taken that the cheese by all these systems is made with starter. Where this is not done, the evening's milk is ripened either by keeping it at its natural heat, or after aeration, by raising the temperature and then keeping it covered until sufficient acidity is produced to ripen the bulk in the morning.

$32°C$

When the starter is used, the evening's milk, after careful straining, is cooled as quickly as possible to 70° F. This is done by running the milk over a refrigerator, which also aerates it and gets rid of any cowy odors. With a jacketed tub or vat, cold water is run round the jacket until the milk is sufficiently cooled. Where this is impossible the milk must be cooled in small quantities by being placed in cold water; or another way, fill a warmer (where one is available) with cold water and allow it to stand in the centre of

$21°C$

the bulk of milk in the cheese tub, change the water in it occasionally. Naturally the first two methods are by far the best especially where a large quantity of milk is treated, but where there is only 40 or 50 gallons the other two ways are quite workable.

The milk must be constantly stirred to prevent the cream rising and forming a stiff layer on the surface, especially the first hour after it is in the dairy, as this is the time when cream rises most rapidly. In the morning, the cream should be skimmed off and either mixed with the warm morning's milk, if it has come in, or gently warmed by holding it in warm water until the temperature is 90° F. If the cream is well stirred and poured back into the vat or tub through a strainer it will mix thoroughly with the bulk of milk. When the cream is only stirred in, it does not mix, but later becomes churned on the surface, and is never caught in with the curd in the coagulation, and is eventually lost in the whey.

As soon as the temperature of the bulk of milk has been raised above 70° F. the starter may be added, the proportion varying according to, condition of the milk, (if acid less) time of year, strength of starter, and proportion of morning's and evening's milk, if more of the latter less starter, as even when cooled at night milk will always gain a certain amount of acidity.

Sufficient starter should be used to make the milk acid enough to rennet in 1½-2 hours, so that the whole process, from renneting until the cheese is in the press, takes from 5½ to 6 hours. The quantity of starter varies from ¼ to 1%; the latter amount is necessary in the colder periods of the cheese-making season.

The question of leaving the starter in the milk for a long period before renneting is of the utmost importance in the production of a mellow, leafy curd in the later stages. It is found in practice much better and safer to add a small quantity of starter and leave it in a long time than to add a large quantity and rennet soon after. The starter organisms being put into milk at a suitable temperature for their growth, become acclimatized and overcome or at least predominate over, any injurious organisms that may be present. The milk is more evenly ripened and the production of acidity in the later stages is more regular, and thus fast cheeses are not so likely to occur.

The morning's milk can be added at any time, whether in bulk or as obtained, if milking is close to the Dairy. When the whole quantity is in the tub, it may be heated to setting temperature, 84° F. in warm weather, 85° F. or even 86° F. in cold and where there is no means of keeping the temperature of the tub equable.

A test is now taken for the acidity either with the acidimeter or rennet test (see Chapter IV on Tests for Acidity). The amount of acidity necessary varies on different farms, and according to the time of year, and can only be found by experience, by the acidimeter from .2-.21% lactic acid, and by the Rennet Test 19-21 secs. In some cases less than the above and in some more, may be required. It is advisable to wait until sufficient acidity has developed before adding the rennet as ½ hour now will save 1 hour in the later stage of the cheese. The proportion of rennet is again, a variable quantity, on some farms 1 part to every 4,000 parts of milk, on another 1 part to every 8,000 or even 9,000 parts of milk. Taking the proportion of drams of rennet to gallons of milk, it may vary from 1 dram to every 3 gallons, to 1 dram to every 6 or 7 gallons, but sufficient should be used to bring a curd firm enough for cutting in 45-50 minutes from the time of adding the rennet.

(For calculation of proportion, see Chapter VII on Rennet.)

The rennet should be diluted with 4 times its bulk of pure cold water previous to being added to the milk, as it thus assists in a better mixing with the whole, for if the concentrated extract comes in direct contact with the milk, it starts coagulation as it falls and an uneven curd is the result. This can be easily seen where people are in the habit of adding rennet by teaspoonfuls directly to the milk, the curd when ready for cutting is hard in some places and soft in others, and thus curd is damaged and wasted. The maker should well stir in the diluted rennet for 3-5 minutes then cover the tub and leave for 15-20 minutes, returning later to stir the cream in before the milk actually begins to coagulate. This period will be found to be almost regular on individual farms, when the acidity and the rennet is the same. Thus on some farms the milk always begins to curdle in 20 minutes (the most common period) but on another it may take 25-30 before beginning, and yet the curd will be ready to cut in 45-50 minutes. Great care must be taken not to stir when the milk has begun to coagulate or the curd will be spoilt, but judgment can soon be obtained. The bubbles made by moving the surface disappear slowly when curdling begins. If cream is allowed to rise, it will not be enclosed in the casein and will be lost in the whey, the fat if not in the whey will eventually come out when the cheese is put to press, neglect to stir it in also causes a soft floating curd which will possibly produce a mottled and discolored cheese. Old-fashioned makers turn the top of the curd over with a skimmer when the cream rises believing that it will then eventually go into the curd, but this is not so, repeated tests taken of the whey show that the whey is just as rich as if the top had not been so treated. The only way to have all the cream in the curd is to keep the milk moved up to the point of coagulation.

The curd is ready for cutting when it breaks cleanly after inserting a finger and starting a small cut with the thumb. The curd is now cut into small tubes with either the American vertical and horizontal knives, or a diagonal knife, or a shovel breaker (see Chapter III on Appliances). The first gives the best results in that the curd is cut sharply without breaking into small cubes, and there is very little loss of fat or curd in the whey when they are skilfully used. For an oblong vat, the vertical knife is used first, cutting lengthways and across and then the horizontal in the same manner. If the knife blades are close together this is sufficient, but with wide blades it may be necessary to cut again. For the case of a round tub, the curd is first cut round the edge of the tub, and then starting with a small semicircle at the edge of the tub about the size of the blade, the knife is worked across the tub both ways, with both knives. The diagonal knife cuts into diamond-shaped pieces, which is not quite so good as the former as the sharp edges of curd are more likely to break away into crumbs when stirred later on, but it is a decided improvement on the breaker, and is used in the same way as the American knives only twice over, both for the oblong and round tub. The breaker when used in a similar way to the American knives and in careful hands need not cause such a loss of fat and curd, but usually the curd is stirred about and smashed instead of being broken by it. The way to cut a curd properly can only be learnt by experience.

The curd is now cleaned away from the sides and bottom of the tub either with the hands or a rubber squeegee and the cutting continued until fine enough. At this stage the difference in the various systems is observed. For Candy's the curd is fairly small, about the size of peas, for Cannon's decidedly larger (small beans) and in the Scotch smaller than either. The whey now begins to separate and the curd must be kept moving or it will mat together. This is best done with the hands as the curd is in a very soft condition at this stage and requires gentle treatment.

The curd is stirred for 10-20 minutes according to the condition, as it becomes firmer heating may begin for the scalding process. A bowlful of curd should always be drawn from the tap and returned to the tub as this will otherwise be softer than the remainder when drawing off the whey.

The method of scalding depends largely on the kind of appliance in use.* With the jacketed-oblong vat, or round tub the turning on of the steam into the water in the jacket, gradually raises the temperature. With oblong-jacketed vats and water-jacketed tubs where there is no steam, hot water is poured into the jackets, a more laborious but decidedly easier way than some. The overhead heater requires more work than either of the above, as in addition to the ladling up of the whey into the heater there is an extra vessel to clean. Where there is a plain tub, without either steam or water-jacket, it is necessary to ladle out whey into another vessel (the

* See Chapter III on Appliances.

size according to the quantity of milk dealt with) and to lift the vessel, or warmer, as it is called, into the copper, heating the whey up to 120°-125° F., and then slowly pouring it back into the tub to scald the curd. With both the overhead heater and the warmer, it is advisable to employ two scalds or the curd will be cooked too rapidly. To estimate the necessary temperature to heat the whey in order to bring up the contents of tub to scalding temperature, a definite proportion of the whole is taken out. The difference between the temperature of the tub and the heat required will be the number of degrees the whole has to be raised. This figure, multiplied by the proportion taken out and the result added to 84, will give the temperature to which it is necessary to heat the whey in the heater or warmer.

Thus :—if the contents of the tub are 82° F. and the scalding temperature required is 90° F. the whole must be raised 8°. If there are 50 gallons in the tub and 10 gallons of whey are taken out to heat, that is $\frac{1}{5}$. 8 × 5 = 40 + 84 = 124, then the whey taken out must be heated to 124° F. to raise the temperature of the whole to 90° F.

The temperatures of scald for the different systems vary; with Cannon's a low scald is employed usually 94°-96° F., sometimes lower, this is done with two separate scalds of 88°-90° F. and the second 94°-96° F.

The Scotch method is one continuous scald at the rate of one degree in three minutes up to 98°-102° F. With Candy's use a high scald 100°-104° F. with two separate scalds.

With each method the time taken for the scald is about 45-50 minutes, but the degree of firmness of the curd when pitched is very different. When Cannon's curd is cooked through and springy to the touch it is allowed to settle and mat. The Scotch curd is stirred until decidedly firm and shotty while Candy's is intermediate.

The curd is then allowed to settle until sufficient acidity has developed for the drawing off of the whey. The Cannon curd is taken from the tub in a comparatively sweet condition .15-.17% acidity and very moist; this causes the rapid development of acidity in the later stages, which is checked by the cutting and turning afterwards. It is taken out in convenient sized blocks, put into cheese-grey cloths (the number according to the quality of milk dealt with) which cover the rack on the cooler. It is tied up in bundles and one is put on top of the other and a pan over them, upon which a weight of 28-56 lb. is placed according to quantity. The curd is cut into 2-3 in. cubes, 10 minutes after, and put back as before, 10 minutes later it is again cut into rather smaller cubes and put back in bundles. It is now turned every 15-20 minutes according to the rate of acidity until ready for grinding.

The Scotch curd when taken from the tub is in a loose, shotty condition with a high acidity .19-.2% it is shovelled out on to a coarse strainer cloth covering racks on the cooler, and stirred until sufficiently dry, then piled to one end and allowed to mat, the cutting later on is only in large blocks and it is piled two deep each time, remaining so until ready for grinding.

This method is of the greatest assistance when dealing with tainted or gassy milk as the stirring and aeration of the curd after drawing off the whey tends to a great extent to get rid of any odor, and if the curd is again aerated before vatting, a slight taint may eventually disappear.

The Candy curd when taken from the tub in small blocks, is springy to the touch and shows .18-.19% acidity. It is packed closely together sideways on the cooler, 15-20 minutes later the blocks are cut through and again packed, sometimes two deep. After another 15 minutes (according to acidity) the pieces are cut into small cubes and piled with a cloth between the layers. These layers are subsequently turned over at varying periods, until the cheese is ready for grinding. With this method, the curd remains longer on the cooler than in the others.

Some makers vary this by cutting the curd into thin strips. An adaptation of it is of great service with a quick cheese as the small cubes can be spread over the whole of the cooler, the curd is cooled rapidly, it dries quickly, and the speed of acidity is checked. The writer's method of procedure is the same as far as the above up to the time of scalding, a continuous scald is employed (unless an overhead heater is used) taking about 45 minutes. The temperature of the scald varies, principally according to the soil. It is therefore advisable to have some idea of the nature of the soil before starting cheese-making on a strange farm. On impervious clays or water-logged land a high scald up to 102° F. is necessary and even on a heavy loam 100°-102° F. may be required according to the amount of lime in the soil. With a loose sandy soil, 88°-90° F. is often found sufficient, especially in the early spring of the year when the milk is poor as the curd rapidly becomes granular and shotty, and will not mellow in the later stages if a higher scald is used. The same applies where there is a very thin layer of soil over a rocky formation, and upon such land in the writer's estimation it is most difficult to make a first-class cheese. Soils upon red-sandstone and limestone formations usually require an intermediate scald as do also peat lands.

The curd when thoroughly cooked is springy and shotty to the touch (i.e.—if a small quantity pressed together in the hand, and then tossed in the air, will readily come apart) and may then be settled and a test taken. The amount of acidity necessary at this stage to form an elastic curd that will work well in the later stages is usually .16-.17% by the acidimeter or $\frac{1}{8}$ in. to $\frac{1}{4}$ in. on the hot iron according to time of year, etc. The curd is allowed to mat for about 10 minutes and is then pressed with the hands or with a piece of wood or tin, into a solid mass. It can be easily done in an oblong vat where the curd is merely pushed back from the tap end at least half-way up the vat; with a round tub more care is required, the curd is pressed gently to the centre all round the tub, and then drawn towards the side next the operator, who turns it in the whey until it is in a round compact mass, that can be moved about with the hands without breaking. A bowlful of whey should then be drawn from the tap and returned to the tub carefully on the top of the curd and the curd is left until sufficient acidity has developed and the

PLATE E.—CURD PILED IN TUB.

(See page 49)

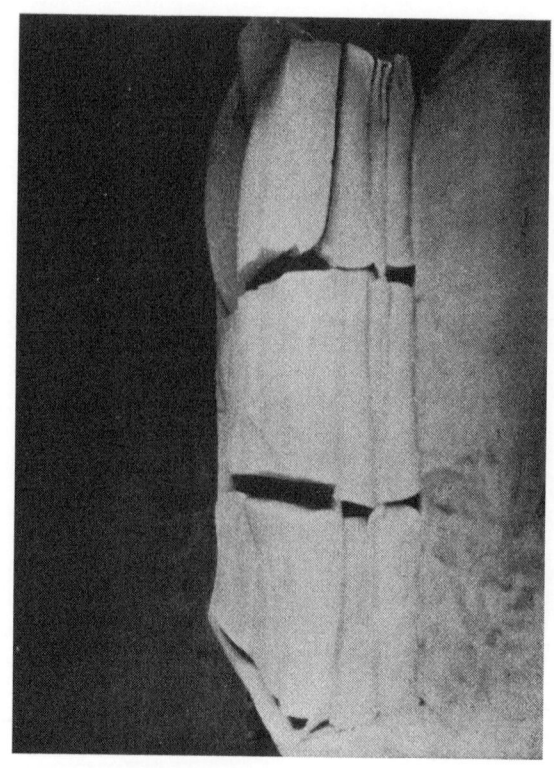

PLATE F.—CURD ON COOLER. FIRST PACKING.

(See page 49)

whey is then drawn off. If the curd has been well pushed up, there should be very few crumbs of curd in the sieve at the tap. Some makers manage so well, that it is hardly necessary to use a sieve at all.

See Plate C for the appearance of the curd in a round tub after the whey has been drained off. The curd is then cut as in Plate D and the pieces packed on the square in the centre, placing the portions, so that the result is a square of two thicknesses. (See Plate E.) In a vat the curd is merely halved either in the whey, or afterwards and one half placed on the other. It is then covered and left for 15-20 minutes according to acidity, if working quickly leave it only 10 minutes. The time between any of the turns must be shortened or lengthened according as the cheese works quickly or slowly. The square of curd (either in the vat or tub) is now cut in equal divisions twice each way making 9 pieces. Each piece is again cut through horizontally making in all 18 pieces and it is then removed to the cooler. In this method, this is the only cutting required. A cloth is spread over the rack at one end of the cooler and the curd piled in 3 layers of 6, thus $6 \times 3 =$ total of 18 pieces. (See Plate F.)

A cloth is laid between each layer to prevent the curd from matting and to assist drainage, the middle cloth being used to test for the whey drainings while the curd is on the cooler. Twenty minutes later it is re-piled in layers of 3 six deep ($3 \times 6 = 18$). (See Plate G.) After another 20 minutes it is again piled in 9 layers of 2 ($9 \times 2 = 18$). (See Plate H.) The curd by this time has pressed itself into thin sheets and at the next turn these are placed one on top of each other; when dealing with a large quantity fold the sheets of curd double. (See Plate I.) The curd may now be left until sufficiently acid for grinding. If it is working slowly, the curd should be turned say every $\frac{3}{4}$ hour. To assist drainage on the cooler when the acidity is developing rapidly a rack and weights 28 lb. may be put on the curd. On land where it is difficult to obtain a good texture these weights are found of great assistance, though not invariably necessary.

At the turning it is well to place the outside curd and in the early stage to turn outside edges, to the middle, so that the curd is even all through.

The curd when ready for grinding should (see Plate J) be in thin sheets and resemble chamois leather, velvety to the touch, smooth in texture, the joining of the granules of curd hardly discernible. The curd is leathery and can be peeled off in thin strips and tied in knots, a small portion bitten between the teeth resembles indiarubber. The amount of acidity necessary on different farms before grinding, varies according to the amount of curd dealt with, the season of the year and the temperature of the atmosphere. On some occasions .6% will be enough to give press drainings of .95%-1.05%, on another as much as .9% is necessary. This is a matter which the cheese-maker will be able to judge by testing the press drainings daily.

The object of grinding or milling the curd, is to reduce it to such a size that the salt can be evenly mixed and to assist in the removal of the moisture when in the press; it is only by breaking up the curd that it can be pressed into a marketable shape. (For curd mill see Chapter III on Appliances.) After grinding the curd is thoroughly stirred with the hands for 10-20 minutes to aerate and assist in the mellowing as the action of the air softens the curd, doing away with any harshness. It is then piled and allowed to remain in a heap, covered with a cloth, to further mellow and mature before the salt is added; at this stage it develops a smooth 'velvety' texture which has a great influence on the flavor of the finished cheese.

The curd must never be left exposed to the air at any stage, as it will become yellow and cause a highly-colored cheese, to which the dealers at the present day very much object. Salting must not be hurried unless the curd is too acid, nor must the temperature be above 80° F. when the salt is added, thus an open and tough texture is avoided, as well as one of the causes of bitterness in cheese. Salt is used at the rate of 1 oz. to every 3 lb. curd or 2-2½ lb. salt to every 112 lb. curd, where the curd is weighed; in large dairies the quantity is calculated according to the amount of milk. In spring 1 oz. to every 3 gallons of milk will be enough, but should the curd be moist or too acid, or later on in the season in July, August and September more salt is necessary, 1 oz. to every 2¾ gallons. To reckon roughly, for every 100 gallons milk, allow 112 lb. curd and divide that quantity by three, which will give ounces of salt required. Sufficient salt should be used to produce a good flavor, some dealers have a preference for either more or less and it is advisable to consider this fact; in some districts, e.g. the North, all articles of food are considered more palatable with plenty of salt. When the salt has been well stirred in, the curd should be piled and left for 10-15 minutes for it to dissolve, and when the atmosphere is below 70°-75° F. and above 65° F. it may be vatted, if vatted at a higher temperature there will be excessive loss of fat in the press, if too low the curd will not mat or join together when pressed and may eventually crack or break in the ripening room. If a portion of the curd is squeezed in the hand, just before vatting a rich fatty whey should exude, but there should not be sufficient moisture present to leave the cooler wet after its removal. Many makers like to see the whey just begin to run from the vat when they are finishing vatting.

The vats or moulds may be lined either with coarse strainer cloth or cheese-grey. The cloth is used dry when a test is to be taken of the press drainings, but otherwise a damp cloth is found more convenient as it clings to the side of the mould better. A long-shaped piece put round the mould does not cause so many creases as when a square is used and the cloth can be more easily pulled up after the cheese has been put to press some hours, obviating the necessity of turning it at night when there is every likelihood of breaking a heavy cheese by inexperienced hands. Some makers use bags to fit the vat or mould and these are only pulled up when the cheese is turned, and never taken off again, but the cheese removed to the ripening room with them on. A small square of cheese-grey is put on top and the bag folded neatly over, making as few creases as possible. A laced bandage is then put over this. Some think the fat that exudes during pressing, greases the rind of the cheese and that the cloth keeps it in better condition later on, this may or may not be the case, there is no doubt that where a large quantity of cheese is dealt with, a tremendous saving in the labor of washing cloths is effected, and the method certainly should be convenient for factories, as each cheese would then have a fresh cloth and there would not be the risk of contamination by sour cloths. The curd should be firmly pressed into the moulds and the wooden follower put on and the cheese removed to press, at first with screw pressure only, then gradually tightened as the cheese shrinks until the bar or chain of the press is lifted. A test of the whey drainings should now be taken, and should contain from .95 to 1.05% lactic acid by the acidimeter, never higher, otherwise as the curd is moist, it will develop too much acidity in the early stages of ripening; in some seasons, less is necessary than others. There is a tendency at the present day for cheese vatted at the lower acidity to be more popular so long as it is full-flavored. The bar of the press should be kept screwed up until the evening, the wooden follower is then removed and the cloth well pulled up all round and the top made smooth, and the tin follower put on with the wooden one so that there will be a good surface in the morning. Some makers turn the cheese at this stage and wring the cloth out of warm water before putting back to press, but this is not essential. 5-10 cwt. pressure is now put on, if 112 lb. cheese the latter is necessary. Next morning the cheese is taken out, turned, and greased one end and half-way down the sides, a cap put on and a bandage of cheese-grey put round the sides. The other cap being loosely laid on top when the cheese is in the vat. It is now put back to press with 15-20 cwt. pressure. In some parts it is customary on the first morning after making to bath the cheese in water at 120° F. in order to seal the coat and form a nice rind. The cheese is suspended in the water by the four corners of the cloth and held for 2-3 minutes according to its

Cheddar Cheese-making.

size. It is then slipped back into the mould and left for 1½-2 hours, and when cooled and drained, is changed into a smooth dry cloth.

The second morning after making, the cheese which has been capped one end, is well greased the other end and side, the bandage being taken off to do it. The second cap is put on, the bandage returned pinning it in place without putting the pins into the cheese. In the case of a cheese that has been bathed the previous day, it is greased all over, and both caps and bandage put on at the same time. The application of melted grease (pure lard) assists not only in helping to put on the dressing cloths, but to form a good rind and at the same time prevents excessive evaporation. A trial with 12 well-greased cheese, showed that there was an increase of 1 lb. in weight in the ripe cheese over those made on the same day, from the same amount and kind of curd that received no grease at all. The pressure must now be increased to 1 ton to 1¼ tons and the cheese is left until next morning when it is taken out, the pins in the under-band removed, a laced-roller or 'drawn on' bandage put on, and the cheese taken to the ripening room.

The laced-bandages can be made either with worked lace-holes, or with a stout hem strengthened on the edge of each end with a piece of string, and this is then laced up with a strong needle. In any case a piece of folded paper or cardboard should be put under the lacing to prevent a mark on the coat of the cheese. A roller bandage must be put on evenly, not tighter in one place than another, or marks will show on the rind. The 'drawn on' bandages are very convenient where all the cheeses are made one size, these are sewn up beforehand, exactly the size of the cheese, and drawn on when the cheese comes out of press. For this bandage, it is well when the second cap is put on to leave the corners outside the under-bandage to prevent rucking. Naturally a cheese when taken from the press should be bandaged immediately or it will swell at the bottom and cause difficulty in bandaging. The whole treatment during the three nights and two days the cheese is in the press, should be such that a strong and yet at the same time thin rind is obtained, which will prevent cracking and excessive evaporation during ripening. If the cheese is allowed to crack flies may gain access.

The presses should not be in a draughty or over-heated place, as the former causes cracks and the latter great loss of fat. The ripening room must be kept at an equable temperature 58° F.-65° F. In the hot weather it may be necessary to hang blinds outside the windows, as the heat on the glass causes a rise in temperature. In the cold weather, warm either by steam, or hot-water pipes, or a stove or lamp. The room should be ventilated to prevent excessive growth of mould, but no direct draught on the cheese.

The cheese must be turned daily for at least the first fortnight after it is taken to the cheese room or it will ripen unevenly, afterwards every other day is sufficient. The outer bands may be removed from smaller cheese when 5-6 weeks old, but dealers prefer to have them in the under bandages, otherwise they have to reband them at their stores. If the under-bands are returned their total weight when taken off the cheese is deducted from the weight of cheese, if kept they are usually paid for in the weight of cheese, so that it is actually in practice immaterial to the cheese-maker.

The effect of different systems of make on the finished cheese, is, if the cheese is a good one of its kind, difficult to discern. Originally the Cannon make of cheddar was supposed to be fatter, quicker ripening and with not quite such a lasting flavor as the Candy, while the latter, slower in ripening was apparently a leaner cheese but excellent in flavor and keeping quality. Both of these systems are inclined to produce a too highly colored cheese for the present-day market. This no doubt is due, especially with Candy's method, to the curd being cut in such small pieces and thereby exposed to the effects of the atmosphere, which rapidly causes a discoloration or darkening. Cheese kept in blocks and closely piled will be paler in color though made from the same milk, than one by either Cannon or Candy's system.

TRUCKLE CHEDDAR.

The difference between the making of truckles and large cheese is very slight; the main alteration is in the pressing of them. It is usually found best to scald rather lower 1-2 degrees and to settle the curd in a softer and sweeter condition. The turns, etc., on the cooler are the same as for large cheese, but the curd must be ground earlier and in a rather softer condition, giving press drainings from .9 to .95% acidity. The cheese should be put to press with chain pressure only and the same evening turned. Some makers grease one end and put on one cap and bandage the first evening. This may be done, or both caps and bandage put on next morning.

In the evening the cheese should be put back to press with 2-3 cwt. pressure, no further weight being added while they are pressing. The following afternoon, about 24 hours after vatting, they are taken from press, and will then have a nice close coat and texture without being hard. On taking from press the bandage is stitched down the side and the cheese is ready for the curing room, without any additional bandages.

LITTLE CHEDDAR.

A little cheese weighing just under 2 lb. can conveniently be made in a small dairy of one or two cows, and will be found much more profitable than if the same milk were made into butter. These cheese are useful for home consumption and are a convenient size for selling retail. Very few appliances are necessary as they can be made in a milk-setting pan or butter-trendle. Three gallons of average milk will make two small cheese. The vessel containing the evening's milk should be held in a pail of hot water and the temperature raised to 90° F. This is then strained into the pan or trendle, which has been made thoroughly hot with scalding water. The vessel is covered and kept in a moderately warm place until next morning. In warm weather the natural heat of the milk will be sufficient to ripen it during the night. The morning's milk should be heated sufficiently, so that when added, the whole is brought up to 85° F. A teaspoonful of rennet, mixed with water, should now be stirred in; the pan is then covered and left for 45-60 minutes. The firmness of the curd will much depend on the warmth of the atmosphere. When of a 'junket-like' consistency it is cut both ways across with a carving-knife, then again slanting both ways to make diamond-shaped pieces. A skimmer or ladle is now used and passed backwards and forwards, starting near the surface until it is cut through to the bottom. Cutting is continued until the curd is the size of peas. It is then allowed to settle 5 minutes and after putting a piece of coarse cheese-cloth over the top, enough whey is taken out to heat for the scalding (see calculation for method of scalding large cheddars). It is best to scald these cheese to 95° F. Pour back the hot whey gradually into the pan stirring gently with the hand. This process must not be hurried, or the curd will not be cooked evenly through. It is preferable to take 30 minutes from the time the curd is settled until the temperature is raised. Continue stirring with the hand until the curd is firm but not hard. Settle for 10-20 minutes and ladle off as much whey as possible, straining it through the coarse cheese-cloth. Spread the cloth containing the crumbs over a bath and carefully tip the curd without smashing it into the cloth. Tie up into a tight bundle and turn over on the knot, cover and leave 20 minutes. Open out and cut into small cubes (2 in.) tie up and again leave 20 minutes. Open, pull cubes apart, and tie up bundle as before. The curd can now be left longer periods when the cheese works slowly, but the bundle should be opened every $\frac{1}{2}$-$\frac{3}{4}$ hour and the pieces pulled apart. When a distinct acid smell is discernible, a test must be taken. This is done by heating an ordinary flat-iron and using as for the hot-iron test. If the threads draw $\frac{3}{4}$ in. the curd must be broken up with the finger into pieces the size of cherries and about 3 oz. of salt well mixed in and it can be moulded. Small moulds are made for the purpose similar to those for large cheddar,

CHEDDAR CHEESE-MAKING.

or small Caerphilly vats with removable bands may be used. Another plan is to divide the curd up into small cheese in an ordinary truckle vat, by putting a tin follower in between each layer of curd. Press firmly into the moulds and put to press. The after treatment is similar to that for truckle cheddar.

CHAPTER VI.

TAINTS AND FAULTS IN CHEESE. THEIR CAUSE, PREVENTION, AND REMEDY.

TAINTS AND BAD FLAVORS in cheese are due to the following causes :—

1. GENERAL UNCLEANNESS.—(*a*) The impure atmosphere of the byre while milking is in progress. (*b*) The drippings from the clothes of the milker or from the body of the cow, during bad weather, when milking is carried on in the open. (*c*) The splashes of manure on the pail which sometimes find their way into the milk. (*d*) Neglect to groom the cow's body, to wipe or brush from the udder particles of manure, dirt and loose hairs. Cows often wade in stagnant water and stir up the mud on to their udders, they break down the edges of running streams, contaminated perhaps with sewage from neighboring cottages and farm-houses; the trampling on the edges causes the rushes to decay and to form slime, particles of this slime become attached to the body and udder of the cow, and are rubbed off later into the milking-pail. (*e*) The use of dirty stools, spans, and tyes: the milker handles these as he goes from cow to cow, dirties his hands, and washes them in the milk. (*f*) Dirty methods of wet-handed milking; the milker wets his hands with the milk to soften and moisten the udder and so washes off dirt adhering to it, the slime made, may drain over the back of the hand into the milk. (*g*) The wearing by the milkers of same clothes as those used for the dirtiest occupations on the farm. (*h*) Smoking while milking.

2. THE USE OF DIRTY AND IMPURE WATER for the cows and for the washing of dairy utensils.

3. FOODS.—The leaving of foods in the byre during milking. A firm belief still prevails in some districts that various pastures, etc., taint milk and prevent the making of good cheese, but it is a debatable point, as conclusive evidence has not been obtained to prove it. Many such taints entirely disappear when strict cleanliness is observed and it is therefore not unnatural to suppose that were the milk always obtained in the cleanest possible way, and care taken to prevent outside contamination afterwards, it would not become tainted. Garlic, which abounds in some fields, and is luxuriant in growth in May and June, sometimes causes a taint; the question is.—Does the onion smell pass through the cow's system into the milk, or does the milk take up the odor from the cow's body or surroundings during milking?

4. MILK ALLOWED TO STAND UNSTRAINED in the byre after milking absorbs odors very readily while warm, and injurious organisms contained in the milk will increase rapidly with a warm temperature. We are still hoping for the day when cow-sheds will no longer be the source of contamination that so many are at present, but until the time that hygienic cow-byres are the rule and not the exception, the only solution of the difficulty, is, to remove the milk as soon as possible from the fetid atmosphere caused by insufficient ventilation, overcrowding, broken and cracked floors and general bad drainage.

5. THE MIXING FRESH WITH OLD MILK in the same drum or churn and allowing it to cool naturally in an impure atmosphere.

6. THE USE OF CRACKED AND WORN UTENSILS.—Sour milk gets under the joints and soldering.

7. POOR TRANSPORTATION FACILITIES.—The carting of milk from the fields in rusty trunks and churns.

8. THE MIXING OF NEWLY-CALVED COW'S MILK with the bulk.

9. THE USE OF BAD STARTERS.—Sour or stale milk kept over for the convenience of cheese-makers, sour whey and whey-cream and badly prepared home-made starters.

10. UNSUITABLE DRAINS FOR WHEY AND WASTE WATER.—In some cheese-making dairies a whey drain is under the tap of the cheese tub, in others it leads from the whey-lead in the dairy to the piggeries. Both these are a constant source of taint, as the bad odors from the piggeries come up the pipe, and are absorbed by the milk and the curd in the dairy. A drain under the cheese-tub must be trapped, so that clean water can remain in to prevent odors from rising. With the drain from the whey-lead the stopper must only be removed to allow the whey to run off, immediately after cleansing, then it must be firmly corked again. It is better to have the whey-lead in a separate room or 'lean-to' house.

11. UNSUITABLE BUILDINGS. Too close to manure yards.—Insufficient ventilation, both in dairy and cheese-room, in the latter case causes the cheese to ripen unevenly and bad-flavored cheese is the result.

12. 'TEART' LAND.—Some lands cause taints owing to the presence of magnesia in the soil and a high percentage of nitrogen which has a forcing effect on the grasses. The taints no doubt are due to the fact that on this land the cows scour and the milk is more easily contaminated with the manure.

13. SICK COWS and cows suffering from udder troubles.—The following diseases are liable to taint the milk.

INFLAMMATION OF THE UDDER causes the milk to appear like curds and whey, and sometimes tinges it with blood. All the secretion should be discarded until the cow is in normal health again. For if mixed with the bulk, the whole will be tainted and cause a cheese that will ferment even during the making process, and that later in the ripening room will leak and be unsaleable.

COW POX.—The pox ripens forming a hard scab which if care is not taken may fall off into the milk. Teats should be dressed with carbolized oxide of zinc, and the milking done very carefully with dry hands, to prevent contamination. It is best to milk into a pail over which a fine strainer cloth has been tied.

SORE TEATS.—When cows remain outside during the whole of their milking period and are milked with wet hands, exposure and keen winds often cause chapped and sore teats. They are very painful to the animal during milking and the scabs, as with cow pox, may get into the milk. The above precaution should be observed in this case.

TUBERCULAR COWS.—Any cows which appear to have small hard lumps in the udder that can be felt when milking, must immediately be isolated and a sample of the milk taken for examination for tubercular organisms. Milk from tubercular cows mixed with the bulk will cause damage over a wide district, difficult to estimate. Such cows should be always milked by a specified milker who between milking each cow must wash his hands in some strong disinfectant.

PREVENTION OF TAINTS.

1. Clean methods must be the rule in every operation, in the byre during milking, or in the dairy. All stale food should be removed from the troughs and the manure scraped up previous to milking. No litter or fodder must be shaken immediately previous to milking, as the organisms will be in the atmosphere and will later drop into the milk. The cow's udders and flanks should be freed from particles of manure and the udder wiped with a damp cloth before milking commences. The clothes of the milkers must be specially for that purpose, and must be clean, as also the hands. The cows should be milked dry-handed as far as possible, this having been proved to be the cleaner method. Wet-handed milking is excellent when carried out properly, but with dry-handed milking, even if the cow's udder and the milker's hands are not clean, the result is not such dirty milk as would have been the case with wet-handed milking. Milking machines, when brought to a state of perfection, should produce the cleanest milk possible as there is no risk of outside contamination, but unless these machines are made so that they can be thoroughly well cleansed they may be a great source of taint. All utensils, pails, churns, sieves, and

cloths, etc., must be kept scrupulously clean and scalded daily. Stools, spans, tyes, etc., should be washed at least once a week.

2. All sick cows should be isolated and their milk kept apart and tested, to see if it is normal, before being mixed with the bulk.

3. Cows must be given only pure water to drink. Many taints in dairies have entirely disappeared where the cows have only had access to water dipped into troughs and have been unable to wade in the mud, as they otherwise would; a special drinking place made with a firm foundation where they go down to drink is a great advantage, even then in the hot weather the cows stand in the water, contaminating it with their manure, and thus impurities find their way into the milk from their flanks and udders.

Pure water only must be used for washing utensils.

4. All foods liable to give a strong odor must be fed in small quantities and immediately after milking, cabbages, turnips, etc. The food must not be prepared in the byre.

5. The milk as soon as obtained from each cow should be poured through a cloth (tied over the top) into a churn, the vessel being outside the byre in a pure atmosphere. Cheese-grey is suggested at this stage, as the average milker will not usually have the patience to pour milk slowly through a fine cloth; the froth prevents the milk from draining through rapidly. This preliminary cloth will get rid of the main portion of large dirt and thus hinder the development of a great many injurious organisms.

6. As soon as possible after milking the milk should be strained through a fine strainer cloth (flannelette) and aerated to get rid of the cowy odor and in the case of evening's milk cooled below 70° F. to check the growth of the organisms and the souring of the milk during the night.

7. Warm milk should never be mixed with stale, the higher temperature is sure to encourage souring.

Cheddar Cheese-making. 63

8. All utensils must be examined regularly to see there are no crevices under the solder or brass gauges, where dirt or stale milk can collect. The handles of milk pails, milk bowls, skimmers, etc., should be solid so that no milk can collect and become stale. Wooden utensils should never be used for milk, unless they are boiled after being well washed.

9. In the case of drums with tightly-fitting lids, that go down on to the milk, care should be taken that there is no moisture on the top before removing the lids, or it will drain into the milk.

10. No milk from newly-calved cows should be added to the bulk under 7-10 days. The milk of some cows becomes normal quicker than that of others. It is advisable to heat a small quantity of the milk and if the milk does not curdle it may be mixed.

11. Where there is an inside drain in the dairy either for whey, or waste water, even if it is trapped it should be cleaned thoroughly daily and pure water left in. Drains outside the dairy are always preferable, the liquid being conveyed to them by open drains or removable gutters that can be easily cleaned.

12. All dirty and stagnant water should be fenced off to prevent the cows from wading in it, and clean water dipped for drinking purposes.

13. Cows should never be put into a field where there is an excessive growth of garlic (in May and June). In the prevention of taints it is safer to mow such a field as the odor is sufficiently strong to be taken up by the milk.

14. Pure culture starters only should be used for cheese-making and they must be renewed when of a doubtful nature. When a taint appears the above points must be thoroughly gone into. In a dairy where milk is bought, a sample of each supplier's milk should be kept in a glass jar (that has been put in boiling water to kill all germs in it) at a temperature of 90° F. for 24 hours. If on examination it appears normal, free from gassy holes and strong odors, then individual cows

must be examined in the same way until the source of the taint is discovered.

FAULTS IN CHEESE.

SPONGY OR HEAVY CHEESE are caused by an organism, *coli communis* usually found in manure and sewage. Also found largely in fowl manure. It is therefore unadvisable to allow fowls to be near the milk-pails, etc., or the dust from the dried droppings will in all probability be blown on to the pails and so contaminate the milk. The organisms gain access to the milk from the manure and produce a gas which, in its effort to escape from the cheese, causes small holes in irregular masses. Its presence may be detected by a strong odor or by sponginess only. The action of this organism tends to check the development of acidity, and the acidity present is not very apparent unless tested for. When a curd appears gassy a cheese-maker should develop acidity as quickly as possible and constantly test as its action is uncertain. Sponginess may also be caused by milk coming from a cow with a chilled or inflamed udder, and also by the use of inferior rennet.

ROPY MILK often appears in the spring of the year. The organisms causing the trouble are found in the udder when the cows are suffering from inflammation, and it is said to be also due to second-cut clover, tares, sanfoin and trefolium. The milk may be drawn out in long strings; fortunately there is no harmful result on finished cheese from it, but it is very difficult to eradicate when it once makes its appearance. Soap and soda appear to encourage its growth but weak solution of acid will get rid of it.

FAECAL TAINT.—This taint is due to contamination by manure and appears faint at first but later on develops more strongly. If sufficient acidity is developed before vatting and the curd thoroughly well aerated it may be got rid of and be hardly noticeable in the finished cheese.

FLOATING CURD is sometimes caused by feeding too much on cotton cake, but its chief cause is using milk from

PLATE G.—CURD ON COOLER. SECOND PACKING.

(See page 49)

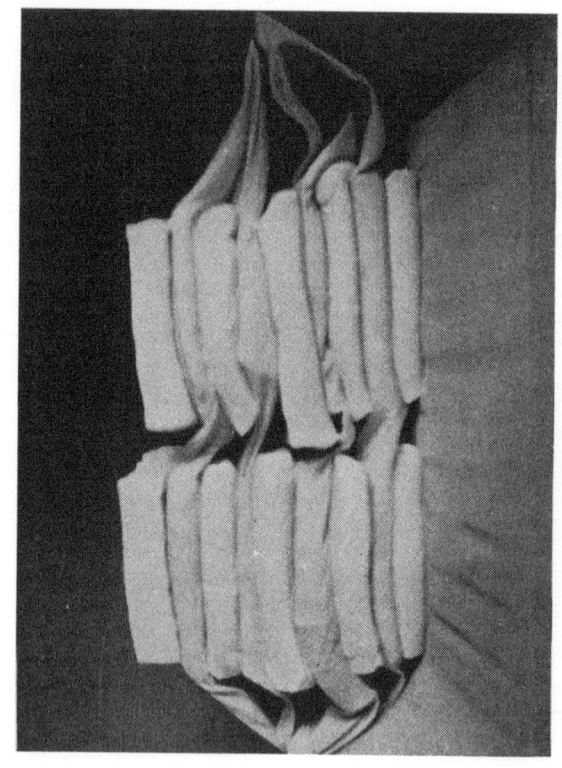

PLATE H.—CURD ON COOLER. THIRD PACKING.

(See page 49)

CHEDDAR CHEESE-MAKING.

freshly-calved cows. It contains a high percentage of organic matter and also albuminoids which readily ferment. New milk must not be mixed with the bulk of milk for cheese-making until 7-10 days after calving. When in the cheese-tub, the curd produced from such milk will, after the addition of the rennet, rise to the surface of the whey when cut, and there will be great difficulty in separating the moisture from it. The curd throughout will lack body, and the resulting cheese will be misshapen, leak and heave in the cheese-room and be altogether unfit for sale.

VINEGAR TAINT.—According to work carried out by Mr. F. J. Lloyd in Somerset, this taint is due to an organism found in cow manure and produces in the curd a smell closely resembling vinegar. The acidity develops rapidly as in an ordinary over-ripe cheese. The curd must be scalded higher and be made drier before vatting. The natural development of acidity will often thus be checked and the curd should then be closely watched to note the correct time for grinding. The cheese when ripe has a stingy flavour and is much like an over-acid cheese. This taint does not now appear to be as prevalent as in former years.

BITTERNESS IN CHEESE may be caused by the excessive use of catch crops in feeding and by chilling the curd on the cooler, and by the use of worn utensils. It may also be caused by a micro-organism which is especially active in a cheese that has been vatted with insufficient acidity. It does not appear in the earlier stage of ripening, but later when the cheese is ready for market and usually gets worse as time proceeds. Colostrum and the milk from cows suffering from udder troubles will produce bitterness.

Cheese cured in cold store often becomes bitter if suddenly changed to a high temperature.

AN OPEN OR HOLEY CHEESE is due in many cases to being put up too sweet. The cheese then contains a large amount of milk sugar upon which the bacteria present act producing small quantities of gas causing small round regular holes in the body. If free from any objectionable odor it may be concluded that the fault is due to mismanagement in the making, not to tainted milk. Scalding too high and too rapidly, and irregular cutting, leaving too much moisture in the curd, using milk too soon after calving, excess of green foods and brewer's grains, all tend to cause an open-bodied cheese.

RED AND BLACK SPOTS ON RIND of cheese. The former appear occasionally and will grow luxuriantly on over-acid cheese. Black spots denote the presence of the harmful mould mucor, which is found in manure and the appearance denotes uncleanliness somewhere. Black spots may also be caused by the presence of iron in the milk, which has come there through rusty churns and buckets, etc. The slightly sour milk causes the iron to go into solution and thus get into the cheese.

MEALY OR DRY TEXTURE due to too great development of acidity before running off the whey, or allowing the curd to become too dry and crumbly by over-scalding or by stirring in the whey.

TOUGH AND CORKY TEXTURE.—If coagulation period is too long, the curd becomes tough. Other causes are too much rennet, insufficient acidity before drawing off the whey, general lack of mellowness in the curd before grinding, besides a want of acidity in the finished cheese, the curd being too dry to mellow.

SOAPY, WAXY, OR PASTY texture is due to the curd being cut too large, using milk from newly calved cows, insufficient cooking of the curd in the whey, not enough acidity in the whey at grinding and putting to press too warm.

HARD, DRY CHEESE, NOT CUTTING FAT caused by poor milk, too high temperature in making and scalding and too high acidity, and excessive loss of fat during making.

RANK FLAVOR is due to excessive feeding of cabbage, etc., bad rennet, worn and dirty utensils and the use of new milk.

WEAK FLAVOR is caused by foods given to the cows, the development of too little acidity in the process of making, and the curing of the cheese at too low a temperature.

CHEDDAR CHEESE-MAKING.   67

LEAKING CHEESE in ripening room is caused by too little acidity before renneting, the use of insufficient rennet or too low temperature at renneting, insufficient scald, vatting too soon and pressure applied too quickly, vatting too acid and keeping at too high a temperature during ripening. A leaking cheese should be pierced with a knitting needle to get rid of excessive moisture or it may go rotten in the middle. The loss of fat in the ripening room is due to too high temperature.

MOTTLED OR DISCOLORED cheese are caused by improper mixing in of the cream from the evening's milk, and also, allowing the cream to rise on the coagulum at renneting. Also unless the starter is strained, lumps of curdled starter become entangled with the other curd. If coloring matter is used it should be of good quality and added at setting time, otherwise certain organisms in the milk liberate carbon dioxide and hydrogen and the latter gas possesses bleaching properties, causing discoloration.

The curd during the whole process of manufacture should never be exposed to the influence of the atmosphere or it will darken in color.

The popular cheese on the market at the present time is of a very pale color, this is not always possible to obtain in the early spring months of the year, when the cows are freshly calved and their milk contains a large proportion of lactochrome or the coloring matter of milk. Also the fresh grass in the spring tends to produce a much larger proportion of coloring matter than do the dry foods fed at other times of the year.

CAUSES OF SOFT CURD are insufficient acidity before renneting, insufficient or weak rennet, temperature too low, very rich milk, presence of an exceptionally small quantity of lime-salts in the milk, heating too rapidly and not high enough and insufficient stirring and the curd being too acid in the whey.

LOSS OF FAT IN CHEESE-MAKING.

There is the greatest loss of fat in the spring and early summer months, due to the fact that on most cheese-making farms the cows are all newly-calved in the spring when their milk contains a larger proportion of the oily fats. The first flush of grass also tends to produce a higher proportion of the soft fats which readily come away from the curd during the process of cheese-making. Rough treatment throughout the process of making, in the stirring of the evening's milk, in the mixing in of the cream, in stirring in cream at renneting, at cutting and stirring of the curd in the tub, with excessive cuttings on the cooler and grinding at too high a temperature and putting to press when above 75° F. All cause excessive loss of fat. In the making up of over-acid milk there is additional loss of fat as the curd when quickly formed does not so readily enclose the fat globules.

DIFFERENT METHODS OF TREATMENT.

A CURD SLIGHTLY OVERSTIRRED WHEN RENNETING should be cut very gently rather larger than usual and should be stirred with care for a shorter period and not be scalded so high; the moisture will thus be kept in it and the curd will not become too dry.

A curd slow in developing acidity should be cut larger, scalded lower, and left in the whey longer. It should be kept warm throughout, if in a tub, by covering with cloths, if in a vat, hot water may be put in the jacket.

GASSY OR TAINTED curd should not be allowed to mat in the tub or vat, but be taken out loosely and well stirred before getting into a mass. It must again be well aerated (20 minutes) after grinding and odors can then sometimes be got rid of.

CURD LACKING IN MELLOWNESS. — If not mellow although sufficiently acid for grinding, the curd should be ground and the salt added and then well stirred for 10-15 minutes, put into a heap at the end of the cooler covered and left for 20-30 minutes, then well stirred again before vatting.

Cheddar Cheese-making.

Curd Too Moist when Ready for Grinding.—Spread cloths on racks all over cooler and grind the curd on to the cloths. Stir well and salt, again stir and spread well out and cover with cloths, leave 15-30 minutes before vatting, a great deal of the surplus moisture will then have drained away.

When Excess of Rennet has been Used.—Cut earlier and heat sooner. Do not raise temperature of scald so high, and settle earlier. The whole process should be worked so that the curd does not become too dry before acid enough for grinding.

CHAPTER VII.

RENNET AND ITS SUBSTITUTES, SALT AND COLORING USED FOR CHEESE.

Rennet is the agent used in cheese-making for the coagulation of the casein of milk, when this takes place, the curd encloses the fat globules, separating the milk into curds and whey.

Rennet is obtained from the fourth or digestive stomach of the calf and the vell or lining is soaked in brine to extract the ferment. Rennet can be bought commercially in three forms (1) liquid (2) tabloid (3) powder. Of these the first is by far the most convenient form for use, but in hot countries, where rennet is required only occasionally the other forms are valuable.

The ferment of rennet acts best in an acid medium, it is for this reason that ripe or acid milk curdles more rapidly than sweet, and its action is greatly retarded by an alkaline solution, which explains its slow effect on milk containing such preservatives as borax or carbonate of soda. Any alkaline salts present in the milk must be in solution, thus boiled milk will not coagulate with rennet, boiling having caused the lime-salts to become insoluble.

Originally it was thought possible to obtain rennet only from very young and milk-fed animals, but recent experiments at Reading prove the contrary, as satisfactory results have been obtained when using either the fresh or dried vells of calves up to two and three months old. Years ago farm-house cheese-makers made their own rennet from the dried vells, but as the commercial extracts became more common, and were found more uniform, besides effecting a great saving of labor, the home-made methods were discarded and the commercial extracts came into general use. This was in pre-war days before the imported foreign vells became scarce. Recently rennet has become so expensive that cheese-makers have begun to consider the advisability of either making their own or using a substitute. Experiments in the preparation of home-made rennet, have been carried out at Reading by Mr. Todd and Miss Cornish, for some time past and some preliminary information was published in the Journal of the Board of Agriculture Vol. XXIII No. 5, August 1916. In this paper a detailed description of the method employed there, is given and persons wishing to make their own rennet should carefully follow these directions. The results so far have shown that a cheese-maker taking proper care, can make sufficient rennet during the winter (if vells are procurable) to keep good through the cheese-making season if kept in a suitable place. Several of the large firms that supply rennet are attempting to cope with the shortage of supply and to this end are putting up factories and buying all procurable vells, therefore there should be a supply of commercial rennet, but makers of home-made rennet may have difficulty in obtaining vells. As we are dependent on some coagulating agent for cheese-making, it is well to obtain satisfactory information one way or the other as to the cheapest and best supply, before the season commences.

Before using fresh rennet, however obtained, it is always advisable to test its strength, the simplest test is by the rennet test (see Chapter IV Tests for Acidity). Good commercial rennet should coagulate fresh milk in 33 seconds, and this time may be taken as a standard to compare a fresh rennet and to form a guide before adding it to the milk.

There are various methods of calculating the proportion of rennet to use, but however done, sufficient should be added to bring a nice tender curd in 50-60 minutes. The amount will vary in different districts and according to the time of year, quality of milk, acidity of temperature, and atmospheric conditions. If a longer time is taken for coagulation, the process of the cheese is delayed and there is no advantage. The simplest way of reckoning the quantity, is to use one dram to

72 CHEDDAR CHEESE-MAKING.

so many gallons of milk; thus with one dram to every 4 gallons of milk, it is merely necessary to divide the quantity of milk by 4 and the result gives the amount of rennet required in drams. Glasses to measure ounces and drams are more easily procurable than other kinds. A more accurate measure is obtained by using an ounce or 2-oz. glass divided into 100 parts of an ounce. With this glass the proportion of one part of rennet to so many parts of milk is calculated. The gallons of milk are multiplied by 160 to bring them to ounces and the result divided by the proportion of rennet to be used. Thus 100 gallons milk × 160 = 16,000, this divided by 8,000 (that is if the rennet is to be used in the proportion of 1 part rennet to 8,000 parts of milk) gives 2 which is marked on the glass as 200. Therefore with this proportion, a cheese-maker has only to double the gallons of milk and this will give the number of parts of rennet to use on the glass. With other proportions calculation must always be made. In practice it simplifies matters to dispense with the noughts and multiply the milk by 16 and divide by 8. Ex. 120 × 16 ÷ 8 = 240 parts on the glass. These accurate measures are difficult to obtain now that glass ware is short, therefore it is well for cheese-makers to be able to compare this measure with the ounce and dram. One part of rennet to 8,000 parts of milk is the same proportion as 1 dram to 5 gallons of milk. When we turn to the other proportions, it is not so close as this, thus for 1 in 7,000 the nearest would be 1 dram to $4\frac{1}{2}$ gallons.

There are still many people who cling to the old-fashioned way of measuring rennet with a teaspoon or egg-cup. This is undesirable and troublesome at any time but when rennet is as valuable as now, an accurate measure may influence not only the quality of the resulting cheese, but the cost and amount of rennet used during the season.

Rennet to keep its strength, must be stored in well-corked, and sealed barrels, or stone jars, away from the light, in a cold dry place. Small quantities for daily use should also be kept well corked in stone bottles away from the light.

RENNET SUBSTITUTES.

PEPSIN.—It was shown some years ago, both in Canada and England, that quite good cheese could be made with pepsin and as there is less likelihood of there being a shortage of this material than of rennet, it may be well to give a few details of its use.

Pepsin is obtained from the stomachs of pigs, it is sold in powder and scale form, the former, owing to its light and deliquescent nature, is not so convenient to handle as the latter. Pepsin prepared by Armour & Co. is sold at such a strength (1 to 3,000) that 2 oz. dissolved in 20 oz. of water is sufficient to coagulate 300 gallons of milk. The proportion required for a definite quantity of milk must be calculated from this and the pepsin accurately weighed. The disadvantage of its being in powder and scale form instead of in liquid is, that the average cheese-maker has not an accurate balance, but if, as has been suggested, a solution can be turned out commercially that will not deteriorate, it will be just as convenient to use as rennet.

After the quantity has been weighed, it is thoroughly mixed with water at 105° F. and it is desirable if possible to dissolve the pepsin at least half an hour before use, the mixture can then at renneting be diluted with water as in the ordinary use of rennet. Individual cheese-makers must find the proportion necessary for their milk. If a certain quantity of rennet is available it may be used in equal parts with pepsin and a very good curd will be obtained.

SUBRENNA.—This substitute, prepared in liquid form by Parke Davis & Co., is convenient for use in cheese-making and as far as is known, has up to the present produced satisfactory cheese, but final and conclusive trials have not yet been carried out. Directions for its use are given on the bottles and it is estimated that it will, like pepsin, be considerably cheaper than commercial rennet, although no cheaper than home-made rennet.

Some cheese made with pepsin and subrenna produced

a higher yield than those made with commercial and home-made rennet, this no doubt is due to the large amount of moisture retained in the curd. This moisture hastens the ripening, and the cheese was ready for market in advance of those made with rennet, the curd being well broken down and buttery. After they were kept a longer period, there was a tendency for the flavor to go off, this no doubt being due to the excessive moisture causing other fermentations to take place after ripening. It would therefore seem that for early spring cheese, substitutes such as these, might be of great value in producing a cheese for the early market, but for long-keeping cheese, the curd must be put up drier than would be necessary with ordinary rennet curd, if the flavor is to be unimpaired in the later stages of ripening.

SALT USED FOR CHEESE.

The salt should be pure and of the best quality, for much good cheese is spoilt by the addition of inferior salt, which causes discoloration in the finished article. A simple mechanical test for purity, dissolve some in a glass of hot water, and there should be no discoloration or sediment. Salt containing magnesium chloride or gypsum in any but minute quantities produces a bitter flavor in the cheese. The quality of the salt may be judged by its appearance. It should be clean, white, and have a silky look. To test chemically dissolve $\frac{1}{2}$ oz. of oxalic acid crystals in 4 oz. of an equal mixture of liquid ammonia and water. Take the salt to be tested and dissolve a tablespoonful of it in water, and place in a glass test-tube, say 8 in. long by $\frac{3}{4}$ in. in diameter. If on pouring in about a tablespoonful of the oxalic solution, a cloudiness appears in the liquid, it denotes the presence of sulphate of lime or gypsum. Salt when added to the curd suppresses lactic acid formation, and the acidity appears definitely checked, its after effects are to improve the flavour of the finished cheese, making it more easily digested and increasing its keeping qualities.

The salt, when it comes in contact with the fresh cheese, attracts moisture and is converted into a saturated brine, thus promoting osmotic processes in the cheese. This liquid, penetrating into the cheese, causes another liquid, the whey, containing the milk-sugar, lime, and phosphoric acid, to flow out. The more of the brine solution penetrating, the more therefore will the whey flow out, and the percentage of water will be reduced and the cheese made drier. The amount of salt present in different cheese varies. In cheddar it is about 2.7%.

CHEESE COLORING.

Coloring, when used, should consist of some harmless vegetable material, free from foreign taste and odor, and with an appetizing appearance. It should be easy to apply and besides possessing strong coloring properties, should be a reasonable price in proportion to its true value.

There are two kinds in common use:—

1. An alcoholic soda solution of annatto.

2. An alcoholic solution of saffron. The former imparts a red-yellow color and is used mostly in England, America and Holland. The latter, a yellow, is used in South Germany and Switzerland principally.

Annatto is obtained from the seed pods of a plant called *bixa orelana,* which is grown largely in South America and East and West Indies. The seeds, which are about the size of wheat kernels, are found in two rows inside the hairy pod. These seeds are covered with a yellowish red, resinous matter, which is dissolved with various substances, and the liquid coloring thus obtained is used for coloring milk immediately before adding the rennet in cheese-making.

The saffron solution is made by dissolving 1 gram of saffron in a 20 c.c. mixture of 10 c.c. common spirits of wine and 10 c.c. distilled water. This is shaken up in a roomy bottle and allowed to stand for 4-5 days at ordinary room temperature. It is again shaken and finally filtered through muslin before using.

Coloring before being added to the milk should be mixed with 4-6 times its quantity of water and poured into the milk in bulk, just before adding the rennet and thoroughly stirred in. If put in too early the action of the starter is liable to bleach the coloring and produce a mottled cheese.

Aniline dyes produce a non-appetizing color, and are injurious to the health. The question of the use of coloring depends entirely on the district where the cheese is made. If the market demands a colored cheese, it is best to suit its taste. In later years there has been a tendency for a much paler cheese and few makers use coloring except in the early spring, when the cheese would otherwise be white.

CHAPTER VIII.

THE RIPENING OF CHEESE. STORAGE AND PACKING FOR EXPORT AND MARKET.

The process of cheese-making is analogous to that of the digestion of milk in the stomach, except that in the latter case the complete process takes place in about 4 hours, while with cheese it is extended to several months while the cheese is ripening.

During the ripening of cheese, the firm, tough and elastic curd, which is insoluble, is changed into a digestible and soluble substance. The cause and manner of these changes are still not definitely known, many clever investigators having quite contrary opinions. In hard cheese ripening, it is thought that both bacteria and enzymes are necessary as a typical cheese cannot be made without these agents being concerned. Experimental cheese made with chloroform to check all microbial action showed that the digestive process was still continued. Again, if bacteria are the only agents concerned, why is there no change in the proteids when they are grown in sterilized milk? Bacteria no doubt assist normal ripening by the production of lactic acid which hastens and assists the action of enzymes in rendering the casein soluble. The casein is gradually broken down by stages into more soluble substances, albumoses, peptones and amido compounds and ammonia and carbon-dioxide are formed; while these processes are going on the water is getting less and the fat greater. The changes in cheese are slower than in the alimentary canal, due to the fact that the ferments have solid substances to work upon and the temperature is lower than in the alimentary canal.

Galactase, the natural enzyme of milk, assists in breaking down the proteids, but its action is not essential as cheese can be made from pasteurized milk, which process destroys the action of enzymes.

Lactic acid bacteria predominate over all other microorganisms (99%) in the early stages of ripening. They were at one time thought to check putrefaction in ripening but are not much present in the later stages; they convert any sugar remaining in the cheese after 3-5 days into lactic acid. Lactic acid bacteria favor the curdling process and the expulsion of the whey and help in the matting of the curd, they also assist the action of the pepsin in rennet. Thus rennet acts indirectly in cheese-ripening by the addition of the pepsin and by incorporating more moisture which hastens the ripening process.

During the fermentation of the lactose or milk sugar into lactic acid, alcohol is produced, and this is thought to play an important part in the production of flavor and aroma by bacteria.

COLD CURING OF CHEESE.

The great advantage of curing cheese in cold storage is the decrease in shrinkage owing to the smaller loss of moisture, as a consequence there is more cheese to sell.

Cheese kept at 60° F. shrinks about 5%.
,, ,, 50° F. ,, ,, $3\frac{1}{2}$%.
,, ,, 40° F. ,, ,, less than 1%.

The cheese produced is creamy, close in texture and of mild flavor. Cheese kept at 25° F.-30° F. requires eighteen months to ripen. A low temperature inhibits the growth of undesirable organisms, but if subjected to a sudden rise in temperature, these organisms will soon develop. The curd produced for cheese to be ripened in cold storage must be dry, or the cheese will be soft and weak in texture. The great disadvantage of cold curing is the slow returns, and expensive artificial cooling machinery necessary.

COLD STORAGE AND PACKING OF CHEESE FOR EXPORT.

Cheese that is to be shipped in cold storage should be kept at a temperature between 50° and 60° F. for 14 days after removal from the press. The cheese may then be waxed to prevent growth of mould during ripening, as this is usually great when cheese is ripened at a low temperature. Waxed cheese do not shrink so much during ripening and there is about 3% increase in yield. The wax aso prevents dryness and rancidity. The thinnest possible coat of wax is best and the cheese should be held in it for 8-10 seconds. Best odorless paraffin wax at a temperature of 200°-250° F. is used. A special vat, including a swing dipper and means for keeping up the temperature, being employed.

The cheese are then drawn out and left to drain over the vat until they can be handled. With small cheese it is usual to cover with a film of parchment, this being pressed on to the cheese.

BRANDING may be best carried out with a mixture of coal oil and lamp black as it does not become blotted.

The cheese are then packed in boxes with plenty of space which should be filled up with insulating material such as asbestos wool to prevent change of temperature. For marketing in England it is usual to send the cheese away in their under-bands packed with straw in round baskets to fit the cheese. These are more easily handled than boxes on rail. When there is a consignment sufficient for a truck-load they are usually packed directly into the truck without being put in either boxes or baskets. Care must be taken that they are well covered with some waterproof material to prevent damage from wet weather *en route.*

CHAPTER IX.

EXHIBITION OF CHEESE. POINTS FOR JUDGING CHEESE. THE KEEPING OF CHEESE RECORDS.

EXHIBITION OF CHEESE.

Although at the present time cheese shows have been abandoned, this should in no way check attention to the preparation of produce for exhibition purposes, for cheese that is good on the show bench is good on the market. With dairy produce in particular, the value is enhanced when special care is given to the appearance. The taste of the general public is influenced to a great extent by the eye and it is always well to remember the importance of first impressions from the judge's point of view. At many of the small local shows this fact is entirely forgotten; if exhibitors would take hints from the larger shows they would materially advance their chance of prize-winning. Uniformity must be one of the first points aimed at when showing cheddar cheese, one inferior cheese will stop what would otherwise be a prize lot of cheese. The cheese to be seen at its best should be even in size and appearance, so that at first glance a judge is pleased. Then, should the method of manufacture have brought about a desirable result, that cheese is sure to figure in the prize list. A crooked cheese with round edges and raised top may be of good quality but it is not of good marketable appearance.

Attention must be given to the appearance of the cheese, as soon as it is vatted, careful treatment in the press being most necessary. The Scotch method of bathing the cheese in hot water (120° F.) the morning after making helps to seal the rind and produces a good

PLATE 1.—CURD ON COOLER. FOURTH PACKING.

(*See page* 49)

PLATE J.—CURD BEING GROUND OR MILLED.

(See page 50)

coat which, when well rubbed with melted grease, softens the rind and prevents any hardness. There is no doubt that a liberal application of grease, goes far to the improvement of the coat. During ripening care must be taken with the turning that the edges do not become broken, and also that the cheese is not in a draught or cracks will result. In bandaging with roller or other bands, the bandages should be put on so that the method employed cannot be detected. The appearance of the rind when the cheese is ripe can be greatly improved with a little judicious scraping and polishing, after rubbing in some grease or oil that will not give any odor to the cheese. If the rind is smooth and unbroken and has not been allowed to mould, the cheese will present a much more attractive appearance.

Competition acts as an incentive to the production of good cheese and if cheese-makers will only go about with open minds ready to take lessons from what they see, the standard of the cheese will necessarily be raised. It actually costs no more, except in time and trouble, to make a good article than it does one of an inferior quality and the extra price obtained for such far outweighs the trouble involved. Prize-winners rarely have any difficulty in selling their produce, therefore all makers should aim at making a cheese capable of taking a first prize and they will then be able to demand a good market price for it.

POINTS FOR JUDGING CHEESE.

There are many different scales of points for judging cheese. The following may be taken as an example:—

Flavor	40
Body and texture	40
Color	12
Appearance and finish	8
Total	100

THE FLAVOR should be mild, pleasing, and full, not strong, biting, or acid. Fine nutty aroma and free from taints.

BODY AND TEXTURE should be smooth and close, free from openness, no moisture visible in any part, dry yet not crumbly, plastic, yet free from stickiness. It should cut buttery on the iron and the plug on the trier should come out nearly solid and smooth. When crushed the cheese should break readily (not bend) down into a smooth greasy mass, when broken across show a flaky break.

COLOR should be pale, even and uniform throughout, no discoloration or mottling and an even color near the rind. In a new cheese there should be a tendency to shininess. Coloring matter when used should be bright and clear.

APPEARANCE AND FINISH.

The cheese should be symmetrical in shape and form, with flat ends or surfaces, and neat edges, level and straight sides not bulging; the size according to market, weight and circumference in proportion. Exceptionally tall or flat cheese have not great market value. Thin skin or rind, transparent, no cracks, springy to touch, smooth surface.

KEEPING QUALITY AND DIGESTIBILITY.

Good cheddar should keep 12 months and should be capable of being sent to any part of the world without damage. The popular cheese at the present time is one that cuts buttery on the iron, having a fine nutty aroma, of pale even color and mild flavor, almost melting when on the tongue. Cheese having a stingy, biting flavor and crumbly texture is more often than not the result of the production of too much acidity in the whey, even though checked later when the curd is on the cooler. A hard dry cheese is produced from milk poor in quality, too high scald and insufficient development of acidity in the whey, the curd never becoming close, leafy, and mellow, but crumbly and hard.

KEEPING RECORDS OF CHEESE MADE.

For the successful production of good cheese a careful daily record is of the greatest assistance; for later, when the cheese has ripened and is offered for sale, a study of the record will show the causes of the best and worst cheese produced. A record is of no use unless kept accurately; it need not be elaborate but should contain the most important stages in the day's cheese-making. The cheese must have either a number or date marked on it when taken to the ripening room; it can then be identified and compared with the records of other cheese treated differently during making.

The main points to observe in the making of cheddar cheese come under the following headings.

> Date (or number).
> Gallons of milk.
> Quantity of starter used.
> Time when starter was added.
> Acidity at renneting.
> Quantity of rennet.
> Temperature at renneting.
> Period of coagulation.
> Temperature of scald.
> Time taken to raise the temperature.
> Acidity before drawing the whey.
> **Periods between turning the curd on the cooler.**
> Acidity before grinding.
> Quantity of curd and proportion of salt used.
> Acidity of press drainings.
> Time of whole process.

CHAPTER X.

RETURNS OBTAINED FROM CHEESE-MAKING. BYE-PRODUCTS, WHEY AND WHEY BUTTER.

RETURNS OBTAINED FROM CHEESE-MAKING.

It is always advisable when embarking on a particular system of dairying, first to calculate the probable financial returns of the same. These returns although they can only give an average or possible result according to circumstances prove of great guidance, and show if the undertaking is likely to be profitable, when compared with other systems of dairying, the difficulty of getting fair comparative results is not sufficiently realized, many failing to look at all sides of the question. Thus we hear that ' the plant for cheese-making is too expensive ' and that milk-selling, whether wholesale or retail, is far the more profitable. With wholesale milk-selling, labor is considerably minimized, but as against this must be put the total loss to the farm of all the constituents of milk; distance from station or factory is an important point, beside the trouble of cooling the milk should cold water be scarce in summer. With retail milk-selling the farm must be in close proximity to a town, or the milk can never be delivered at the correct time. Thus in some districts cheese-making is advisable and at the same time the most profitable undertaking.

Where cheddar cheese is made, the season usually extends from March to October, some makers going on into November. It is estimated on most cheese-making farms, that $4-4\frac{1}{2}$ cwt. cheese are produced per cow from Lady-day to Michaelmas, and where grazing is included 4 cwt. may be taken as the figure. Thus if a cow yields $2\frac{1}{4}$ gallons per day for the 190 days (roughly) from

CHEDDAR CHEESE-MAKING.

March 25th to September 29th that will be 475 gallons. Taking the whole year through, 1 lb. cheese should be produced from every gallon of milk, the richer milk in the autumn balancing the poorer in the spring, thus 475 lb. cheese is roughly 4¼ cwt. per cow per season. To the value of the cheese must be added the value of the whey, if complete returns are to be taken. It is calculated that there are 85 gallons of whey from every 100 gallons of milk used; thus for the 475 gallons milk there would be 403 gallons of whey.

As regards the price obtained for this quantity of cheese and whey, it is difficult in these days to make a definite statement. Before the war 7d. per lb. would have been considered a fair price to average throughout the year, bringing the returns for the 475 lb. of cheese to £13 15s. 5d. to this amount add the value of the 403 gallons whey at ½d. per gallon 16s. 9½d., bringing the total to £14 12s. 2½d. At the present time both the cost of producing milk, and the returns obtained from it have doubled; approximate returns may be taken from the following example. On a dairy-farm where 70 cows were in milk last year during the cheese-making season, the average price, throughout the year for the cheese was 116s. per cwt. This would make the returns for 4¼ cwt. cheese per cow, £24 13s. add to it, the whey, which must now be valued at ¾d. per gallon (403 gallons at ¾d. = £1 5s. 2¼d.) bringing the total return per cow for the season to £25 18s. 2¼d.

WINTER CHEESE-MAKING.

Although having no bearing on the question of cheddar cheese making, it may be interesting to quote here the returns for caerphilly cheese, taken from the same farm as were the figures for the cheddar. During the months of November, December and January, 2,674 gallons of milk were made into caerphilly cheese. From this milk previous to making into cheese, sufficient cream was taken to make butter and for the ordinary use of the household. The returns from the caerphilly cheese averaged for the three months 1s. 7¾d. per gallon, to which must be added the value of the whey, roughly 2,272 gallons at ¾d. a gallon. It will be seen from this that winter-cheese-making, at the present time is decidedly more advantageous than milk-selling.

WHEY as a bye-product, from the average cheese-making dairy is only valuable for its feeding value to animals, in particular pigs. Its actual value lies principally in the large proportion of milk-sugar it contains. When abstracted from it, the worth of the sugar lies in the fact of its digestibility and hence it is largely used in the making of invalid and infant foods. The process of abstraction is too elaborate for ordinary cheese-makers, besides it is necessary for a large bulk of whey to be utilized. Whey at the present time is not given its full value as a beverage, it has long been recognized as a very good drink for invalids suffering from lung trouble and anaemia.

As regards its food value for animals, 2 lb. whey are equal to 1 lb. of skim-milk and 10 lb. are equal to 1 lb. of farm grains, thus fed in conjunction with meals, it is of the utmost service in fattening pigs, producing a meat which when sent to table, never eats as dry as that produced when no whey is used for feeding. It is usually reckoned on a cheese-making farm, that two pigs can be kept for every cow in milk. Whey, when used judiciously, in the feeding of calves and fowls gives very good results.

At factories, where a large quantity of whey has to often stand about in the tanks and is likely to become sour, as a preventive, put the steam pipe in the tank and heat the whole up to 180° F. thus fermentation will be retarded to a great degree.

WHEY BUTTER.

The practice of making whey butter is still largely carried on in cheese-making counties, and must be encouraged now that every article that has feeding value should be saved. The great danger in encouraging the making of whey butter, is that it is liable to cause carelessness in the manufacture of the cheese, the cheese-maker thinking it immaterial if the fat is lost from the cheese so long as plenty of whey cream is obtained. The fact must never be lost sight of—that every 1 lb. of fat increases the cheese 3 lb., whereas 1 lb. of whey-butter is not of the same value as 3 lb. of cheese. With the old-fashioned method of cheese-making it was reckoned to make 1 lb. of whey butter per cow, per week, this we know to be excessively wasteful, as in a 40 cow dairy the best cheese-makers do not produce more than 3 or 4 lb. of whey butter per week, many decidedly less. Since the more up-to-date methods of manufacture have been employed, many people have discontinued saving the whey, but have allowed it to run direct to the pig-geries, and certainly it was hardly worth while when fats were so cheap as they were two or three years ago. Now that it has been proved that making milk butter is not only unprofitable to the maker, but also does not make the best use of the contents of milk, butter obtained from a bye-product may in a small degree take the place of milk butter.

In cheese-making there is always a small amount of fat lost in the whey, and it is this fat that should be recovered for whey butter. The whey should be put into some vessel for the cream to rise, whey-leads are the most useful, as tin is liable to wear out rapidly with the action of the acid in the whey, and old worn vessels, such as copper tubs, etc., cause fermentations, which taint the butter. The whey should be set somewhere outside the dairy for should there be a tainted cheese made one day, the whey from it is liable to taint the next day's produce.

If allowed to remain undisturbed until next morning, a thin layer of cream will have risen to the top and may be skimmed off. This cream is put in a vessel that can be hung or floated on the surface of the copper, or, other hot water and the temperature raised to 150° F. some clean cold water is then added to it, about two or three times its bulk. The whole is then poured into a well-glazed earthenware vessel that has a plug-hole at the bottom, and set in a cool place until next morning.

Remove the plug and run off the water from underneath until the cream comes, and then pour the cream into a pan or pail, that is kept to collect the bulk for churning. The earthenware pot, after being cleaned and scalded is then ready for the next lot of cream.

The bulk of cream should be stirred daily and salt added to prevent it developing a strong flavor. It should be churned at least once a week, and when churning plenty of water must be added to the cream and the butter well washed when in granules. This should produce a palatable article. Whey butter always has a distinct flavor, but this is by no means objectionable if well made and it is certainly superior to margarine and other fats. Economically it is of much greater value used for human consumption than if run off in the whey for the pigs, as they fatten equally well on other articles of food.

CHAPTER XI.

MAKING CHEESE FROM HEATED OR PASTEURIZED MILK.

The object of heating or pasteurizing the milk before making it into cheese, is to have a complete control over the milk supply. Thus if the milk, whatever its source, could be made germ free, and then a pure growth of organisms added to it that will carry out the various requirements of the cheese, a uniform product should be obtained. This should be of the greatest service at factories, where large quantities of milk are bought for cheese-making, but unfortunately skilled labor is absolutely necessary, as irregular heating of the milk, and injudicious treatment later, will have disastrous results.

It was originally thought impossible to make cheese from milk that had been heated to a high temperature, until experiment proved that this was not so. Both the English and American results show that a saleable article can be produced from heated milk if the temperature is not too high. A high temperature gives a cooked flavor, and the curd will not expel moisture, if the temperature is irregular or too low foreign flavors will be the result.

Pasteurized milk when renneted produces a soft flocculent curd, lacking in body and too fragile to be handled, the whey is expelled from it very slowly and the production of acidity is also slow. This is due to the chemical and physical changes which are produced by the high temperature. The lime-salts, which are in such close combination with the casein, become separated and insoluble and the process of pasteurization drives off the carbon dioxide present in the milk, thus the milk does not coagulate so readily when renneted.

The resulting product is more uniform in flavor and more sanitary, although it never attains such a strong flavor as a cheese made from raw milk, but is rather of the mild variety. It will usually stand excessive heat and cold better than normal cheese.

The experiments carried out at the British Dairy Institute, Reading, prove that the most satisfactory cheese is made when the temperature does not exceed 165° F. A higher temperature may destroy more organisms in the milk, but the milk is afterward much more difficult to make into cheese.

To obtain the best results, heating must be carefully carried out in a jacketed vat, and the milk immediately cooled. The milk usually requires more rennet, and the starter used, must be a matter of discretion as the curd usually develops acidity rapidly in the later stages. It also requires a longer and higher scald to get rid of the whey, less solids are found in the whey, and this no doubt is one of the causes of the higher yield. The curd requires to be heavily pressed to assist 'matting' and to prevent as far as possible a loose texture, salt at the rate of 1 oz. to every 4 lb. curd gives an excessively salt taste. The cheese when in the press and ripening-room, must be handled carefully; they are never as tough as when made from untreated milk.

The resulting cheese is softer and more plastic in texture and gives the impression of containing a higher percentage of butter fat. They take longer to ripen but keep well afterwards and produce 5-9% more in weight than ordinary cheese. The flavor is milder and more uniform throughout and there is less risk of taint. Experiments have been carried out in America with satisfactory results, the treatment of the milk there being different, in that, after pasteurization, the milk is brought to a definite acidity with a weak solution of hydrochloric acid. This acid being a natural constituent of the gastric juices is more likely to produce satisfactory results. It was added to the milk from a jet to prevent curdling, the milk being kept moving where it mixed. According to their method, using a fixed amount of starter the acidity is always uniform and the various processes carried out at definite times. This system could not very well be carried out at the ordinary factories in England, as expensive appliances are required and a chemist or some other skilled worker would be necessary to obtain good results. It has been suggested that the way in which pasteurized milk might be of most service in this country for cheese-making would be, to pasteurize only part of the milk that is to be used. For it has been found that if only part of the milk has been heated, the curd, formed from a mixture of it and new milk, more nearly resembles a coagulum than from ordinary raw milk. Thus in factories the pasteurization of the evening's milk would do away with any risk of taint from it; then if the morning's milk were thoroughly cleansed by a dirt-centrifuge, the risk of inferior produce being made from mixed milks would be greatly reduced.

CHAPTER XII.

YIELD OF CHEESE. STANDARD FOR CHEESE. BUYING MILK FOR CHEESE-MAKING.

YIELD OF CHEESE.

The yield of cheese from a definite quantity of milk is influenced by the following conditions :—

1. Time of year. In the spring of the year and early summer, an abundance of fresh succulent grass, causes an increase in the quantity of milk, but the quality is usually poorer, and consequently the yield of cheese from such milk is lower. In the South-Western districts, the month showing the lowest yield is usually May, as the grass is earlier, in the Eastern and North Midland counties, June is found the lowest. The milk will yield only from 94 to 98 lb. of green cheese to every 100 gallons, whereas in the autumn in the months of October and November the yield will be from 108 to 114 lb. per 100 gallons.

2. Length of time the cows have been in milk. In the early part of the lactation period the quality of the milk is poorer than later on, thus on cheese-making farms where the season is extended until the cows dry off, the later part of the time gives an extraordinarily high yield of cheese.

3. Food influences the yield, in that all succulent foods, such as grass, catch crops, etc., and brewers' grains, produce a high yield of milk, of somewhat poorer quality and hence less amount of cheese is made from such milk.

4. Wet weather. It has been noticed that in especially wet seasons there is always a lower yield of

Cheddar Cheese-making.

cheese. This no doubt is due to the quick growth and watery condition of the grass.

5. Rich and poor pastures. It is usually found that rich pastures produce a larger yield of milk, but of poorer quality. Poor pastures produce less milk, but of rich quality.

6. Quality of milk, proportion of fat to casein. The variation in the amount of casein in the milk is fairly regular to the fat and thus the approximate yield of cheese may be calculated from the amount of fat present. There is an average of 2.7 lb. of green cheese for every 1 lb. fat in the milk when of about 4% quality, thus 4 × 2.7 lb. of green cheese were obtained from 100 lb. milk. The highest amount of fat that is lost in cheese-making is in April, May and September (.4%). The lowest is in June, July and August (.33%) whilst with bad workmanship it may reach 1.0% per 100 lb. milk. The loss of casein is greatest in October and June and smallest in April.

7. Method of manufacture. Unless great care is exercised in all operations there may be serious loss during the making of a cheese. Rough treatment of the evening's milk while warm, improper mixing of the cream from the evening's milk, rough stirring of the milk in the vat or tub, not stirring in the cream at renneting, rough cutting and stirring afterwards, all cause the whey to be very rich. It should not contain more than .25-.3% fat; a skilled worker can very often keep it as low as .2%, but with rough usage, the whey will sometimes reach .6-.8% fat. Again if the curd is cut a great deal on the cooler and into small pieces the drainings from the cheese may contain as much as 2% fat when it should never be more than .5%. Grinding the curd too warm and putting to press when above 70° F. also cause the press drainings to be excessively rich.

8. After-treatment during curing. If the cheese is kept at too high a temperature while ripening, there is great loss in weight. The cold-curing of cheese has proved that, by that particular method the loss in ripening is brought to a minimum. 58°-65° F. is quite high

enough temperature for cheddar, above that excessive shrinkage takes place, not only spoiling the yield but also the value of the cheese. In hot weather care must be taken that the room is not warm enough to cause the fat to leak or there will be great waste. The greasing of the coat, and well bandaging of the cheese prevents to a great extent shrinkage during ripening.

LOSS IN PRESS AND IN RIPENING.

It is very difficult to make a definite estimate of the loss in press and ripening. So much depends on the condition of the curd when put to press. The loss in press may vary from 6 to 13% and yet in each case the cheese may be satisfactory, while in ripening it may be from 4 to 9%. The figure that is most important is the final yield of cheese per 100 gallons of milk. Some makers put their cheese to press in a very dry condition and it may possibly not lose more than 6% and when in the ripening room only 4%; but a cheese made from similar milk, and put up with more moisture, will in all probability yield as much if not more cheese, and yet may lose 10-12% in press and .7-8% in ripening.

A rough estimate as regards the yield of cheese from Essex milk was calculated in 1911 and it may be of interest to quote the results here, so that comparisons may be made with other yields. About 12,000 gallons were used on the 178 cheese-making days. The following figures are those obtained per 100 gallons of milk used :—

Month	Cheese Yield %	Loss in Press %	Loss in Ripening %	Total loss %
January	108.6	13.4	7.7	21.1
February	109.7	15.5	9.2	24.7
March	112.1	10.4	5.6	16.0
April	111.8	12.7	6.2	18.9
May	101.4	7.7	5.2	12.9
June	94.8	13.2	8.3	21.6
July	100.2	11.0	7.0	18.0
August	No cheese made. Dairy School closed.			

Month	Cheese Yield %	Loss in Press %	Ripening %	Total loss %
September	102.3	13.8	6.4	20.2
October	108.0	11.5	6.8	18.3
November	113.6	8.0	9.6	17.6
December	113.6	7.9	6.9	14.8
Average for the year	106.9	10.4	7.1	18.6

ADVISABILITY OF A STANDARD FOR CHEESE.

There is a Government standard for milk and butter, but cheese made from skim milk, half milk or whole milk is all put on the same market and it is left to the judgment of the dealer and consumer to distinguish between them. There would be no objection to different grades were they always defined, but as a large proportion of half-milk cheese comes from abroad, it is unfair to the British producer to have to compete in an open market with second-rate produce.

A regular standard should provide a recognized distinction between imported and home produce. If a standardized British cheese were always to be had, it would increase the sale and therefore the output of cheese. The consumer when buying would be protected from having foreign cheese sold him when he demanded British. The standard should be fixed, or the quality of the cheese declared.

Cheese made from partially skimmed milk is a nutritious article of diet, and in many cases the manufacture is to be encouraged where cream, etc., is required for other purposes. But from a cheese-making dairy-farmer's point of view, it is not profitable to skim the milk that is to be made into cheese in any way, however rich. Apart from any question of quality (and rich milk always produces the finer quality cheese) the additional yield of cheese made from whole milk will more than balance the money value obtained, were the same milk made into cheese after the removal of some of the cream for butter. This was proved by a trial of 8 cheese, made from exactly the same amount of milk, but varying in quality. Cream was removed in some cases and added in others, so that the milks differed .5% fat between each, from 1.5 up to 5.0%. It was found that the cheese were ripened, that those made from milk containing about 4% fat were far above the others in quality, and the yield was 11.5% more than with the poorer milks. This trial took place in 1912; the following figures, worked out in 1916 in Somerset, show the loss by skimming at a more recent date.

36 gallons milk, made into butter and skimmed-milk cheese produced:—

	£	s.	d.
12 lb. butter at 1s. 7d. per lb.	0	19	0
18¾ lb. skimmed milk cheese at 6d. per lb.	0	9	4½
Total ...	1	8	4½

36 gallons made into cheddar cheese produced 37¼ lb. 37¼ lb. cheese at 1s. per lb. } £1 17 3

The bye-products were in the two cases approximately of equal value. Therefore a profit of 8s. 10½d. or 2¾d. per gallon was obtained from whole-milk cheese over half-skim and butter-making combined. Whole-milk cheese should be the name applied to cheese made from milk with all its fat in it. The difficulty in fixing a standard is due to the variation in water. By eliminating the water factor and estimating the percentage of fat in the dry matter, comparative figures might be obtained. Numerous samples tested at Glasnevin, show that the percentage of fat in dry matter does not fall below 47. In cheddar the highest and lowest percentages were 53.54 and 48.72 in green cheese and 52.95 and 48.60 in ripened cheese. Taking these figures as a basis it has been recommended that a percentage of 45 should be taken as a limit, below which the dry matter of a genuine cheese should not fall.

The fixing of a standard would prevent the sale of 'filled' cheese, which are made by mixing emulsified

PLATE K.—LARGE AND TRUCKLE CHEDDARS IN CHEESE-ROOM.

PLATE L.—CHEESE *en route* FOR DEALER'S STORES.

foreign fats with skim-milk and then manufacturing the product into cheese.

BUYING MILK FOR CHEESE-MAKING.

In buying milk for cheese-making certain conditions must be laid down between the Vendor and Purchaser if there are to be satisfactory results. Purchasers should insist on inserting a clause in their contracts which allows them to visit the Vendor's premises at any time to see that the milk is produced under the best conditions. Constant inspection would tend to prevent slackness on the part of the producers. There should also be a clause preventing the supply of milk from newly-calved cows until after 7 days. If the milk is to be supplied warm to the purchaser there should be a definite time fixed for delivery, so that the milk can be cleaned by centrifuging and cooled on the purchaser's premises. If cooled before delivery a definite temperature for cooling must be fixed and kept. As regards the quality of the milk the most satisfactory way is, for it to be paid for according to the percentage of fat it contains. This does not necessitate a large expenditure on the part of the purchaser; for a Gerber fat tester, including chemicals, costing about £2 10s. is sufficient. The samples of milk should be taken daily in jars, which contain a small quantity of preservative (potassium bichromate is best, as this does not alter the composition of the milk and its bright orange color prevents risk of the milk being used for any other purpose). The composite sample is tested once a week and an average estimate of the daily fat content obtained, and the price affixed accordingly.

The richer the milk in fat and casein the higher the yield of cheese, therefore rich milk is double the value to the purchaser and the vendor gets the advantage of producing rich milk over poor. Therefore it must be better for both parties to buy by quality rather than by weight or measure.

If we had a simple test for the casein in milk, such as there is for fat, the buyer of milk for cheese-making would be able to pay for the fat and casein content, but as this is not so, we have to fall back upon the fat factor only and this is far more satisfactory than buying by weight.

According to Warrington the product from 100 lb. milk will be as follows:—

	Total Produce. Lbs.	Water. Lbs.	Albumen. Lbs.	Sugar. Lbs.	Ash. Lbs.
Cheese	10.40	3.94	2.57	0.17	0.13
Whey	89.60	83.16	0.83	4.68	0.62
Milk	100.00	87.10	3.90	4.85	0.75

INDEX.

Acidimeter, 31.
Acidity test, 31, 43.
Aeration of curd, 50, 64, 68.
Aeration of milk, 41, 62.
American curd knives, 19.
Annatto, 75.
Appearance of cheese, 82.
Appliances, 12.

Bands, cheese, 51, 53, 54.
Baskets for cheese, 79.
Bitterness in cheese, 65.
Black spots on rind, 66.
Body of cheese, 82.
Boiler, steam, 12.
Bowl, milk, 22.
Branding cheese, 79.
Breaker, curd, 20.
Breed of cows, 4.
Buying milk for cheese-making, 97.
Bye-products, 86.

Calico cheese, 28.
Candy's method, 46.
Cannon's method, 46.
Cheddar moulds, 24.
Cheese-grey, 28.
Cheese-presses, 25.
Cheese records, 83.
Cheese ripening, 77.
Cleanliness, 58.
Cold storage, 79.
Color of cheese, 82.
Coloring, 75.
Consumption of cheese, 2.
Control of acidity and moisture, 29.
Corky texture, 66.
Cow-pox, 60.
Curd cooler, 19.

Curd knives, 19.
Curd lacking in mellowness, 68.
Curd mill, 22.
Curing of cheese, 78.

Dairy, 8.
Dairy buildings, 8.
Digestibility of cheese, 82.
Discolored cheese, 67.
Drains, 60.
Dry texture, 66.

Equipment of dairy, 8.
Essentials for the production of cheese, 2.
Excess of rennet used, 69.
Exhibition of cheese, 80.
Export of cheese, 79.
Exposure of curd to atmosphere, 50.

Faecal taint, 64.
Faults in cheese, 64.
Flannelette, 4.
Flavor of cheese, 81.
Floating curd, 64.
Food of cow, 5.

Gassy curd, 68.
Gerber dirt tester discs, 4.

Hard dry cheese, 66.
Heaving cheese, 64.
Holey cheese, 65.
Hot iron test, 34.

Illustrations, 4, 13, 15, 17, 18, 19, 20, 21, 22, 23, 24, 25, 26, 27, 32.
Importation of cheese, 2.
Inflammation of the udder, 60.

INDEX.

Jacketed tub, 18.
Jacketed vat, 15.
Judging cheese, 81.

Keeping quality of cheese, 82.
Keeping records of cheese made, 83.

Lactic acid bacteria, 77, 78.
Leaking cheese, 67.
Little cheddars, 55.
Loss of fat in cheese-making, 67.
Loss of weight in press and ripening, 94.

Marketing cheese, 79.
Mealy texture, 66.
Method of calculating pressure, 26.
Methods of cheddar cheese-making, 38.
Milk chute, 9.
Mill curd, 22.
Moist curd, 31, 69.
Moisture in curd, 30.
Mottled cheese, 67.
Moulds, truckle, cheddar, 23, 24.

Newly-calved cow's milk, 59.

Open-bodied cheese, 65.
Overhead heater, 18.
Over-stirred curd, treatment of, 68.

Packing cheese, 79.
Pasteurized milk cheese, 89.
Pastures, effect of, 5-7.
Pasty texture, 66.
Pepsins, 73.
Points for judging cheese, 81.
Pond's curd knife, 20.
Portable stoves, 27.
Preparation of dairy, 8.
Preparation of starter, 36.
Presses, double, single, spring, gang, 25.
Prevention of taints, 61.

Press room, 8, 10.
Production of cheese, 40.
Production of pure and uniform milk, 97.

Rack, curd, 19.
Rake, curd, 20.
Rank flavor, 66.
Red spots on rind, 66.
Refrigerator, 27.
Regular supply of milk, 5.
Rennet, 70.
Rennet glass, 33.
Rennet test, 33.
Returns obtained from cheese-making, 84.
Ripening of cheese, 77.
Ripening room, 10.
Ropy milk, 64.

Saffron, 75.
Salt, 74.
Salt-box, 27.
Scalds, methods of, 45, 46, 47, 48.
Scales, 27.
Scoop, curd, 23.
Scotch method, 46.
Scullery, 10.
Shrinkage of cheese, 79, 94.
Sick cows, 60.
Sieve, curd, 23.
Skill of maker, 29.
Slow curd, treatment of, 49, 68.
Soapy texture, 66.
Soft curd, causes of, 67.
Soil, effect of, 5.
Sore teats, 60.
Spongy cheese, 64.
Stagnant water, 7.
Standard for cheese, 95.
Stands for tubs, 16.
Starter, 35.
Steam-block, 27.
Stool cheese, 26.
Storage of cheese, 79.
Stoves, slow combustion, 11.
Strainer cloths, 4.
Strainers, 21.
Straining, importance of, 3.
Subrenna, 73.
Substitutes for rennet, 73.

INDEX.

Tainted curd, treatment of, 68.
Taints, causes of, 58.
Teart land, 60.
Tests for acidity, 31, 43.
Texture of cheese, 82.
Thermometers, 27.
Tough texture, 66.
Truckle moulds, 24.
Tubercular cows, 61.
Tubs, 18.

Use of starter, 35.

Value of cheese as a food, 1.
Vat, 15.

Vats, truckle and cheddar, 23.
Vinegar taint, 65.

Warmer, 18.
Water supply, 6, 7.
Waxing cheddar, 79.
Waxy texture, 66.
Weak flavor, 66.
Weighing machine, 27.
Whey, 86.
Whey butter, 86.
Whey lifter, 9.
Whisk, curd, 23.
Worn utensils, 59.

Yield of cheese, 94.

VIKING RENNET

Is a well-known name in the Dairy Trade all over the World.

VIKING ANNATTO

Is the strongest on the market, giving the Cheese a most beautiful lasting colour.

LOW PRICES.

DAIRY INSTITUTES

May have from us for their own requirements A FREE SUPPLY of our Rennet and Annatto.

British Produce

Write for Samples to the Manufacturers :—

Viking Rennet Co., Ltd.,

19 Clapton Square,

London, N.E.

W. R. BEER,
Pill Farm Dairy,
BARNSTAPLE, DEVON.

The most successful exhibitor of Devonshire Clotted Cream.

Awarded Two Silver and One Bronze Medals at London Dairy Show, also First Prizes at Bath and West, Devon County, Barnstaple, Exeter, Plymouth, etc.

**CREAM, BUTTER, AND EGGS FRESH DAILY.
PRODUCE SENT TO ALL PARTS BY POST OR RAIL.
ALL PRODUCE FROM OUR OWN FARM.**

SATISFACTION GUARANTEED.

DAIRY SALT

Higgin's
'EUREKA'
and
D.V.
BRANDS

As used in Butter Contests at all the principal Shows, also in Agricultural Colleges and Government Dairies.

Ashton, Higgin & Co., Ltd., Liverpool, or Agents.

EDWIN KING,

Ditcheat Factory,

EVERCREECH,

BATH.

Manufacturer of Cheese Cloth, Cheese-grey, made Bandages and Caps, also Linsey.

THESE GOODS ARE SUPPLIED TO THE CHIEF DAIRY INSTITUTES IN ENGLAND.

VIPAN & HEADLY,

Dairy Engineers,

LEICESTER.

Cheese Vats,

Cheese Presses,

Cheese Moulds,

And all Accessories for Cheese-making.

Parke, Davis & Co's
'SUBRENNA'

(Patented)

IS THE MOST SATISFACTORY NATURAL SUBSTITUTE FOR RENNET in the manufacture of Cheese.

: PURE, UNIFORM, :
HIGHLY CONCENTRATED.

One fluid ounce (two tablespoonfuls) is sufficient to curdle 50 gallons of ripe milk or 15 to 20 gallons of sweet milk.

'Subrenna' may be obtained from Chemists and Dairy Supply Houses.

www.ingramcontent.com/pod-product-compliance
Ingram Content Group UK Ltd.
Pitfield, Milton Keynes, MK11 3LW, UK
UKHW041301180426
11947UKWH00009B/614

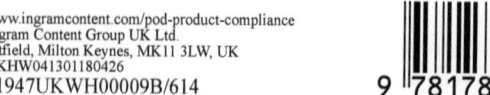